100 Ways to Solve Your Dog's Problems

Sarah Fisher & Marie Miller

100 Ways to Solve Your Dog's Problems

Sarah Fisher &
Marie Miller

D&C
David and Charles

Dedicated to Margaret Fisher (1932–2009), David Fisher (1931–2009), Archie (2002–2009), and to every dog waiting for a loving home.

A DAVID & CHARLES BOOK
Copyright © David & Charles Limited 2009

David & Charles is an F+W Media, Inc. company
4700 East Galbraith Road
Cincinnati, OH 45236

First published in the UK in 2009

Text copyright © Sarah Fisher and Marie Miller 2009
Photographs © David & Charles Limited 2009

Sarah Fisher and Marie Miller have asserted their right to be identified as authors
of this work in accordance with the Copyright, Designs and Patents Act, 1988.

A catalogue record for this book is available from the
British Library.

ISBN-10: 978-0-7153-3207-8 paperback
ISBN-13: 0-7153-3207-4 paperback

Printed in China by RR Donnelley
for David & Charles
Brunel House, Newton Abbot, Devon

Commissioning Editor: Jane Trollope
Editorial Manager: Emily Pitcher
Assistant Editor: James Brooks
Art Editor: Martin Smith
Production Controller: Kelly Smith
Photographer: Bob Atkins

Visit our website at www.davidandcharles.co.uk

David & Charles books are available from all good bookshops; alternatively you
can contact our Orderline on 0870 9908222 or write to us at FREEPOST EX2
110, D&C Direct, Newton Abbot, TQ12 4ZZ (no stamp required UK only); US
customers call 800-289-0963 and Canadian customers call 800-840-5220.

Contents

Introduction

Well done, you deserve praise for two reasons. First you have recognized that your dog needs some help and second, you are reading this book.

We have compiled a variety of common problems that many dogs and their owners experience on an all too regular basis, and have put together a variety of positive, practical, fun and rewarding tips and techniques to help you ensure a harmonious, peaceful and joyful partnership with your faithful friend.

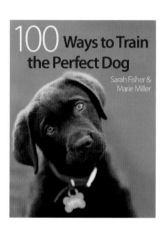

Training your dog

This book follows on from *100 Ways to Train the Perfect Dog*. It is a perfect companion to this publication and will give you many more suggestions and useful information that will enhance your relationship with your dog. We also refer to it at certain points in this book, as it is impossible to include all of the relevant information you may need in one publication. So if you haven't already read this book then we naturally recommend that you do!

Using this book

Although we have listed a variety of common problems, a dog is unlikely to have just one behavioural concern, so you will find that many overlap. It is not possible for us to cover every problem or tip that we have come across in our work, but we have included techniques and ideas that have worked for us. We really encourage you to be creative in the way you work with and bond with your dog.

If you are a new owner and have run into problems you may not have the confidence to work through these exercises on your own. If you are in any doubt about your own skill level it is a good idea to enlist the help of a professional trainer who can help you on a one to one basis.

Give a dog a home

The way a society treats its dogs is indicative of that society as a whole. The fact that so many dogs are looking for new homes, either privately, or through the rescue organisations is probably linked to the problems of the modern world. We live in a throw away society, and one that lacks tolerance, demands perfection, is quick to judge and keen to apportion blame. All this is to the detriment of our dogs.

Of course not every dog in need of a new home is the by-product of an uncaring human. Its owners may have had a change in circumstance such as a relationship break up or move to a property where dogs are not allowed, or they may even have died and an existing family member is unable or unwilling to take on the care of the dog. If they cannot be homed privately these dogs will also find themselves at the shelter, so not every hound that ends up at there has had a bad experience or been picked up as a stray.

Why do dogs develop problems?

Dogs can develop problems for several reasons. Some dogs may have lived with an owner who had too high an expectation of the dog or with someone who did not understand the importance of building a solid relationship with their dog through positive teaching techniques and games that also ensured their companion was learning appropriate behaviours. The dog may have been confused by conflicting messages from different family members and developed unwanted behaviours as a result, or he may even have been an unwanted gift and ignored. He may have been teased or frightened (even by mistake), or become bored and frustrated with his environment. All of these scenarios can create stress in a dog, and a stressed dog can quickly become a problem dog.

Dealing with the effects of abuse

Of course there are tragic cases of dogs being abused, either because people around them were ignorant or deliberately cruel. If you have adopted a dog that you know has suffered from a trauma, feeling sorry for him may hamper his ability to develop confidence and learn new skills.

You need to be aware that your new dog may have already learned some unwanted behaviours in his previous home and you also need to be aware that, contrary to what some people think, dogs do remember and can remember for a very long time. That memory may be inadvertently triggered by contact on a part of their body (by a person or another dog) or by a stimulus in their environment that reminds them of something unpleasant that happened in their past.

Having said that, if you have taken on a dog that had a previous owner you also need to be careful that you don't fall into the 'judgement trap'; for example if a dog goes bananas when a tall, long-haired chap in a hat walks towards him in the park, it does not necessarily mean that he has been abused by someone that fits that description. It may simply be that your dog has never come across anyone that looks like this before, and is alarmed because it is a new experience for him. As confusing as it all may sound, we are merely sharing this information with you to illustrate that nothing is as simple as some people would like to have you think when it comes to dog behaviour; the exercises in this book will enable you to understand and help your dog in a way that is rewarding and pleasant for you both. Always remember that the only thing that can be seen in black and white in the world of dogs is the colour of the coat. (But even then it is worth a second look as the black might be a very dark brown!)

Learn about the breed

Every breed of dog has its own characteristics and traits, so it is important that you read up on the breed or mix of breeds that you have chosen so that you can understand their nature, motivation and requirements. This will help you to know your dog on a deeper level and enable you to find a trainer who can help your dog to reach his full potential, channelling his natural responses in a kind and appropriate way.

Problems can develop for a variety of reasons, but with time and patience the majority of dogs can be helped.

Dalmatians were bred to follow a coach and horses, often for long distances, so they have almost unlimited energy and stamina. If you decide to take one on you must be confident that you will be able to give him lots of exercise.

If you have picked a working breed you will need to ensure he has plenty of outlets for his energy and drive: leaving him sitting at home all day will lead to frustration.

Helping your problem pooch

Most canine problems are usually more of a problem for the owner and society rather than the actual dog itself. Many dog behaviours that may be unwanted and/or unpleasant as far as we are concerned may have actually served the dog well, and unless he is given the motive and the opportunity to learn an alternative behaviour he is unlikely to change. His behaviour may have helped him to feel/stay safe, deal with stress, reduce boredom, control certain aspects of his life, obtain food, keep any potential threat at bay and so on. Naturally, any behaviour that upsets society or other companions in his life can have a detrimental effect on the dog, but it is important that you separate your own emotions from the behaviour that you would like to change and understand that, in order to change a behaviour, you may need to teach him an alternative one instead. You will need to focus on teaching your dog what he can do, rather than constantly telling him what he can't do.

If you have owned your dog since puppyhood and have run into problems, don't be too hard on yourself – it is human nature to make mistakes, and it is a wise person who seeks to correct them. Dogs also change as they mature and you are obviously now on the right path as you are reading this book!

Other considerations

There may be other factors that are influencing your dog's behaviour. Some behaviour, for example, is directly linked to medical conditions that require veterinary support. Pain reduces an animal's tolerance, so it is worth getting a thorough health check for your dog to ensure that he is not suffering from a persistent ear infection, eye problems, thyroid imbalances, a damaged tail, joint problems and so on.

Early experiences (or lack of them) will also influence his ability to adapt to new situations. In order to help your dog you may have to adapt the way that you interact with him, or make alterations to his environment, diet and so on. The more we accept and understand just how much we influence our dogs, the greater chance we have of achieving a harmonious and rewarding partnership.

Layla used to bite hands and feet, but redirecting this behaviour by teaching her to play with appropriate toys instead has enabled her to find a perfect and permanent home.

If you are creative in the way that you work and bond with your dog, you will retain his interest at the same time as helping him to become more confident and secure.

Berserk Human Syndrome

This is a condition that brings about a complete change in posture and behaviour including bracing, clenching of the jaw, holding of the breath, elevated heart rate, and wild eyes. It may be accompanied by strange, if not alarming, vocalisation, slow stalking, sidling, creeping and/or crawling, all of which may be interspersed with frequent bouts of begging. And we are not describing a dog at this point. It usually occurs when there is a specific combination of factors involved such as a dog, a human and a pair of nail clippers, or a dog, a human and topical medications. (It also occurs in the feline world when there is a cat, a human and a worming tablet.) If you recognize this pattern or can relate to this scenario then laugh at yourself, apologize to your dog and carry on reading.

If we look at our interactions with our canine companions through the eyes of our dogs we can develop a greater appreciation of just how inconsistent we as humans can appear to be. The dog does not know that trimmed toe nails or the administration of medications are for his benefit and necessary for his health and wellbeing. All he sees is his usually loving and devoted owner or carer turn into a potential murderer who grabs his collar, his scruff, his foot (or heaven forbid his tail) in a bid to inflict pain and discomfort on him. He also has no clue when your bizarre behaviour is actually going to stop. The calmer and more consistent that you can be when you are trimming nails, towel drying muddy paws, attempting to remove a grass seed from his coat or between his toes, treating minor wounds, cleaning ears or eyes and so on, the less stressful the situation will be for both you and your dog. Follow the relevant tips throughout this book and learn how unpleasant experiences can become less stressful for all concerned.

Understanding your dog's emotions

Dogs are sentient beings with their own thoughts and feelings. They can suffer from anxiety, boredom and depression or be joyful and content. They can be defensive, withdrawn and antisocial, or friendly, engaging and outgoing, and they vary not only in temperament but also in their ability to focus and learn new skills. Dogs have good days and bad days, and are adversely affected by stress, which may lead to them developing compulsive behaviours in order to cope. In short, your dog is as unique and as individual as you are.

Games are an important part of the rehabilitation and training process, reducing stress and building understanding between you and your dog.

9

1 Diet, diet, diet

Your dog's diet will inevitably have an influence on how he behaves. There are countless testimonials to illustrate that dogs fed on a natural, wholesome diet packed with quality ingredients are calmer, more focused and easier to train than those fed on foods containing artificial colourings, additives, and flavourings.

There is now a greater understanding in the human world of the link between poor nutrition and an inability to learn, fatigue, muscle pain, spasms, hyperactivity and perhaps even noise sensitivity, and it stands to reason that this will be true for our dogs. A poor diet will also have a direct impact on health, so buying a cheap, low-grade food can end up being a false economy – the money you save on the dog's dinner could well be spent at the vet's trying to overcome the problems it has created. Be aware that expensive foods can contain ingredients that aren't particularly wholesome or natural – even those sold in clinical outlets. You really need to do your research and find a high quality food that suits your dog, your lifestyle, and your pocket, and be prepared to experiment for a while.

There is currently no legislation that requires manufacturers to state all the ingredients used in commercial dog food, and wording such as 'animal by-products', 'meat and meat derivatives' can cover a multitude of sins.

Remember also that different foods will have different effects on your dog. Some proteins are heating for example, while some dogs cannot tolerate certain foodstuffs such as wheat, beef or even rice. Allergies and intolerances can be linked to skin and ear problems, digestive disturbances and a reluctance to eat, among other problems.

It may also be worth exploring different feeding patterns to address particular problems, such as the research carried out by Val Strong. During stressful periods Val recommends feeding a carbohydrate meal an hour after a protein meal to increase levels of serotonin and induce calm. This could be helpful for dogs that find it hard to settle in the home.

Selecting the right treats

Anything that your dog eats will affect his behaviour for better or for worse, and some dogs literally go crazy after eating certain types of dog treats. Treats will form a valuable part of your dog's training, so you need to ensure that the rewards are as wholesome and as natural as they can be. Look for tidbits made from dried meat or fish, and avoid anything that is brightly coloured, high in salt or full of artificial additives. If you do use other types of products keep a note to see if your dog's behaviour changes after consuming them.

When working with rewards, pick treats that are wholesome and avoid anything brightly coloured, high in salt, or full of artificial additives, as they are liable to contribute to problem behaviour.

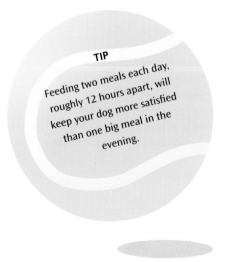

TIP

Feeding two meals each day, roughly 12 hours apart, will keep your dog more satisfied than one big meal in the evening.

Related ideas...   2   8   11   38   39   40

Environment

The environment in which you keep your dog will have a huge impact on his mental, emotional and physical development. A noisy, stressful household that overlooks the individual needs of the canine resident, whether deliberately or inadvertently, is not best suited to any dog, let alone those that require rehabilitation.

There are some simple steps that you can take to ensure that the environment is the best that it can be for your dog. Make sure that he is warm at night. While we are snuggled under a toasty duvet during the winter months we may not realize that our dog is left shivering in a cold kitchen when the heating goes off at night. If a dog is cold he will wake more often and probably urinate more, thus causing problems with house training.

If a dog is noise-sensitive, a bed placed next to the boiler may upset him, and if he is confined to a utility room the noise and movement of the washer or dryer may also have a detrimental effect on his wellbeing. Have a good look around your home and pick a comfortable place where your dog can rest without being disturbed or upset. If he is going to sleep in an indoor kennel, make sure that children or visitors leave him well alone when he is in his crate.

Invisible fences

If you decide to use an invisible fence to keep your dog secure you do need to be aware that in some circumstances, these fences can cause a problem for the dog. Dogs learn by association, and if your friendly dog receives a shock each time he greets visitors as they enter your property he may begin to associate the shock with the arrival of people, and become suspicious or defensive around newcomers. Also, if

If your dog is cold he will wake more during the night and may urinate more frequently, causing problems with housetraining. Make sure he has a cosy bed; for added warmth he could also wear an indoor coat.

the fence is anywhere near his resting place in the house he may get a shock when he is asked to lie in his bed, and if you take your dog out in the car he may get a zap as you cross the boundary if you forget to remove his collar before he gets in the vehicle.

If your dog's behaviour has changed since the fence was installed you may need to re-think its position, and ensure that you remove the collar if he is in the house or accompanying you in the car. It is also important to be aware that other dogs and predators can pass through the invisible fence at will, which can leave your dog vulnerable to attack on his own territory and/or confused.

A quiet, calm household will result in a quiet, calm dog.

Related ideas...   1   5   18   37   41   53

3 Know your dog

It is extremely rare that dogs have just one behavioural concern. Behaviours are linked, and the dog that barks excessively in the car for example is also likely to be over excited at home, overly aroused when out and about and may also be noise sensitive. Understanding your dog's needs, drives and concerns will enable you to take steps that will help your dog to become more confident and calmer all round.

If your dog has more than one behavioural concern it does not mean that you are necessarily going to have to 'train' out each behaviour. By addressing his concerns at home, for example, he may naturally become more settled in the car.

When we work with clients we take a case history and we look at the posture of the dog. We do not need to know everything that has happened to the dog in order for us to achieve a successful outcome, as sometimes there is little information available if the dog has come from a shelter. We look for a link between the behaviours because it helps us form an idea of how we can best help the dog, and it also enables the owners to understand that their dog is not lying in his bed at night conjuring up ways to drive his human companions to distraction the following day.

We may be asked to see a dog because he leaps around on the lead and screams when he sees other dogs, for example. When we meet the dog we may note that he is stiff through the hindquarters, dislikes contact around the hips, has issues with grooming, lacks focus, is frightened of fireworks and finds travelling in a car somewhat challenging. We then may decide to help him overcome his dislike of contact around the hips using TTouch, and to use the clicker and ground work exercises to help him to learn better self confidence when on the lead before we even consider working in the presence of another canine. If we had just focused on the issue with other dogs we may have missed some vital steps in the rehabilitation process.

We encourage you to really study and observe your dog in a variety of situations. Make a list of all the behaviours that your dog exhibits at home and when out and about, however insignificant you may think they are. We recommend you also read *Unlock Your Dog's Potential* by Sarah Fisher to discover the correlation between posture and behaviour.

Skipper is typical of the dogs that come to see us. He had multiple problems, including issues with people, dogs and horses. He hated being groomed and was rigid and tense, showing that he was in a permanent state of arousal.

Sarah started the session with a combination of leading exercises, body work and clicker training. She was able to use TTouches all over Skipper and remove his muzzle once she had established some trust.

The session was broken down into short segments, and Skipper was given plenty of time to play and enjoy walks around the farm.

Skipper was introduced to a fake dog and he reacted in the same way that he does when he sees a real dog.

Sarah rewarded all calm behaviours with the clicker. By the end of the session Skipper's whole demeanour had changed and he was calm and relaxed. He is now able to run freely with other dogs, is good around horses and has made friends with lots of humans, thanks to the commitment of his owners and the on-going help of Garry Hinton, their local TTouch practitioner and trainer.

Related ideas...   6   7   8   9   10

4 Avoid aversive techniques

We do not think there are any excuses for using aversive techniques that rely on pain or fear; it is when understanding stops that violence begins. There are too many unpleasant training methods being promoted in the media and an increasing number of products that inflict pain and discomfort on dogs being sold to unsuspecting members of the public who simply want the best for their dog.

Punishing a dog for unwanted behaviours will add to his anxiety. It is kinder and more effective to use positive reinforcement and reward appropriate behaviours.

If you watched a trainer beating the living daylights out of a dog in a bid to correct unwanted behaviour you would rightly be appalled. No amount of reasoned explanation, or misleading verbal information could distract you from the cruelty you were witnessing. And no one could begin to coerce you into believing 'this is how dogs treat each other in the wild'. Agreed? Well hold this thought. The next time you watch a trainer, observe a class or demonstration or settle down in front of a television programme, turn down the volume and actually watch the posture and the body language of the dog. Is his tail tucked between his legs? Is he urinating? Are his ears pinned back against his head? Is he afraid? Is he flat on the floor with glazed eyes and his tongue lolling as he gasps for breath? You will probably be horrified at what is being inflicted on the dog if aversive techniques are being employed.

Please do not think for one moment that we are telling you that you can improve your dog's behaviour simply by spending your days stroking his ears or threading daisies through his collar while you knit your own nut rissoles and sing around an open fire. Far from it. But there are many positive, productive, and pleasant ways of teaching a dog how to behave and adapt to his environment using compassion and kindness. We have a catalogue of canine clients that range in breed type, age and issues, and we are becoming increasingly disheartened by some of the 'training' techniques extolled by so called professional canine carers. When clients come to us we are often horrified to hear what previous trainers have inflicted upon their dog, and often question where on earth

some of these people are coming from. Do they really think that all the dogs in the world are just quietly biding their time and waiting for their human guardian to err so that they can finally unite in one giant pack and laud it over Planet Dog?

Knowledge

The more you know about dog behaviour and training, the more choices you will have in how you can seek the best help for your companion. Dogs love to be part of the social scene and guess what? They do not think we are dogs. Shutting them in crates so small that they cannot lie down, withholding water, pinning them to the floor, choking them, hanging them, using devices that administer electric shocks if they pull, leave the kitchen or move from their bed will not teach a dog that he is at the bottom of the pecking order in the household. It will alarm, confuse and frighten him, and a quiet dog is not necessarily always the sign of a settled, obedient dog. It can be a sign of a dog that is depressed. The flip side to a depressed dog may be a neurotic or defensive dog, and a defensive dog is a potentially dangerous dog.

The right techniques

The question, of course, is not, 'Should we train a dog?'. Dogs need boundaries, guidance and consistent leadership in order to adapt to the life we have chosen for them. The question is, 'What methods should we use to train that dog, and how can we become effective, kind and compassionate leaders?' Aversive techniques are not allowed in the top UK shelters, and thousands of dogs go on to be successfully rehabilitated and re-homed each year. Dogs trained within the service sector, including seeing-eye dogs, hearing dogs and dogs for the disabled to name but a few, demonstrate extraordinary skills that change the lives of their fortunate owners. In the UK all these dogs are trained with the clicker or other positive techniques. If you inadvertently enlist the help of any trainer who recommends any aversive techniques, dispense with their services and look elsewhere.

Related ideas...   5   7

5 Treat your dog with respect and understanding

The most effective dog people are those who are calm and consistent in their understanding and their handling. They vary the rewards that they use when teaching their dog new skills and use their words well.

Repetitive, short, terse commands will not inspire your dog to work with you and too much talking, even consistent praise, may also switch your dog off. If you are teaching your dog a new behaviour, allow him time to hear what you are saying and to process that information.

Avoid shouting at him, hitting him, dragging or pushing him around and remember to have fun. You want a dog that *chooses* to be with you, rather than one that merely tolerates you because he does not have any other choice. Training at any age and at any stage should be rewarding for everyone concerned.

Imogen has helped her dog, Mattie, overcome her concern about people with patient training, lots of praise and physical contact, and now the pair have a wonderful relationship.

Related ideas...   4   6   7

6 Understand body language

Dogs learn by watching body posture and use their own body language when communicating with other dogs and other species, including humans. Dogs that are poorly socialized may not have had the opportunity to learn appropriate body language, but this is not always going to be true for every dog that has led an isolated existence.

Some dogs, like people, are naturally better at communicating than others. If we do not understand what a dog is saying to us through the movements of his tongue, his eye, his head, his ears, his tail and so on we may inadvertently encourage him to use stronger language such as growling, and biting or may miss the early warning signs that the dog is becoming aroused or concerned which will affect our ability to teach him new responses. As guardians of these incredible creatures, it is wholly our responsibility to understand their non-vocal language as best we can so that we can continue to enjoy the unique partnership that man and dog began thousands of years ago.

Pilot is rather enthusiastic with other dogs!

Lip-licking and scratching are all part of his body language and become more apparent as he begins to learn a little self-control.

Now that he is sitting calmly, his new friend feels more inclined to approach.

Related ideas... 3 5 9

16

Think positive

7

Educating your dog is not just a question of stopping the behaviours that are a problem. Instead you will need to choose alternative behaviours that you can teach your dog so that he has an appropriate outlet for his drives and desires.

Try to erase any memories you may have of your dog trashing your favourite shoes, ruining your dinner party by hurtling across your beautifully laden table in pursuit of a fly, or making you late for an important meeting because he legged it when you were out in the park and you were only reunited after hours of trudging/driving/crying/yelling and a trip to the pound. Avoid focusing on the fact that you may be facing a life bereft of human company because your friends and family cannot cope with the frenzied hairball that has taken up residence in your previously immaculate home and think they have lost you to the Bark Side. Harmony can be restored. All you need is understanding, compassion, patience, a good sense of humour and this book.

Make a list of all the things that you love about your canine companion and all the things that he *can* do, without worrying too much about what he can't do. Too many trainers and well meaning doggy people focus on what dogs need to learn next instead of praising the dog and themselves (or the owner) for what they have already achieved together. Check in with your list if you are ever driven to the point of despair while your dog pursues his mission to seek and destroy.

Fred had many issues when Mina took him on and we take our hats off to her for sticking by him. She has taught him so much and, although he still has a little way to go, Mina should give herself credit for everything she has already done to help Fred.

Related ideas...　　　3　　4　　5　　6

Use a clicker

8

Training your dog using a clicker is a fun and rewarding way of teaching him new and/or more appropriate responses. Use it to mark any behaviour that you would like your dog to repeat.

When working with dogs that lack education we use the clicker not only to mark the alternative behaviours we want the dog to learn, such as sitting instead of jumping up at visitors. We also use it to indicate to the dog that even the smallest shift in his posture, or that split second glance away from the dog, cat, sheep, quad bike (or what ever else has grabbed their interest) is a brilliant and perfect choice, and a really yummy reward is going to follow as a result. This helps the dog to become more thoughtful in his responses and to become active instead of reactive.

We recommend that you read *100 Ways to Train the Perfect Dog* and also Karen Pryor's *Don't Shoot the Dog*.

Sarah uses the clicker when working with Skipper to mark his calm behaviours around people and horses.

Related ideas...　　　10　　11　　12

9 TTouch body work

This system of gentle movements made with the hands and fingers was developed over thirty years ago by Linda Tellington-Jones and is used worldwide by trainers, behaviourists, therapists, veterinarians, veterinary nurses and shelter helpers. It is without doubt one of the best techniques that you can ever learn.

TTouch body work is divided into three groups: circles, slides and lifts, and can be done on any part of the dog's body. It increases circulation and awareness, releases tension and creates a sense of calm. It can teach an animal to accept and enjoy contact, build confidence and reduce unwanted behaviours such as lead-pulling and excessive barking.

This technique has saved the lives of countless dogs deemed to be out of control and beyond help. Our clients are often astounded by the results: their dog is suddenly able to relax, comes when he is called and is more sociable with other dogs and people. Of course, some problems are more serious than others and need time and patience, coupled with the skills of an experienced trainer who can help the dog and his owner on a one-to-one basis using kind and positive techniques.

Body work is fantastic for reducing stress and enables you to be proactive in helping to improve the quality of your dog's life. Here it is used to help Cherry, who has some health problems and can also be a little nervous in new situations.

If a dog is overexcited or tense we use a combination of ground work and body work to help him settle, because a calm dog will find it easier to learn and retain information.

TIP

For further information and detailed descriptions of all the TTouch techniques recommended in this book, read *Unlock your Dog's Potential* by Sarah Fisher (see Further Reading, page 126).

Clouded Leopard TTouch is the foundation for all of the circular TTouches. Curve your hand slightly and use the pads of your fingers to move the skin clockwise in one and a quarter circles. **Lying Leopard TTouch** is similar to Clouded Leopard but uses a slightly flattened hand, so that the contact is made with the area running from the fingertips to the back of the knuckles.

Raccoon TTouch increases circulation, reduces swelling and promotes healing. Curve the fingers more than when performing Clouded Leopard and move the skin in one and a quarter circles with the fingertips, just behind the nails. Perform Raccoon TTouches in the following areas: the base of the ear, the base of the tail, either side of the spine, between the toes and the back of the shoulder.

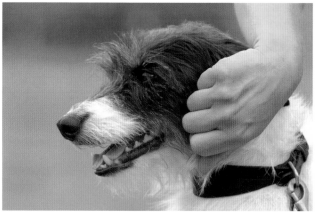

Chimp TTouch is particularly useful for nervous dogs. Curl your hand into a soft fist, keeping your fingers together, and move the dog's skin gently in one and a quarter circles with the backs of your fingers.

Llama TTouch is done with the back of the hand and is great for initiating contact with a nervous animal since they may find contact with back of the hand less threatening. Keep your fingers soft and either stroke the dog lightly or use one and a quarter circular TTouches on the dog's muzzle and body.

Hair Slides are great for long-haired dogs and are also useful for grooming issues and vocal dogs. Gently circle the hair and slide your fingers up to the end of the hair. If your dog is worried by the circular movement do the slides on their own.

Ear Slides release tension around the base of the ears, the forehead and upper neck, and also promote relaxation, helping the dog to settle and stay calm. Hold the dog's ear gently but firmly and stroke from the base right to the tip, moving your hand position with each stroke to ensure that the entire ear is covered.

Mouth Work helps over-sensitive dogs and improves trust. With the dog facing away from you, start by stroking his muzzle and the sides of his face with the back of your hand. If he is happy, continue with Chimp or Clouded Leopard TTouches, supporting his head with the other hand. Work round the jaw muscles and move the upper lip in a circular motion, then slide a finger under the lip and rub it gently along the gum.

Abalone TTouch releases tight ribs and tense belly muscles, and helps with pining, anxiety and digestive problems. Place the flat of your hand on the dog's sternum, with your other hand lightly on his back. Move the skin over the sternum in a circle, then move your hand back slightly and repeat, working along to the belly. You can also use this TTouch all over the body.

Belly Lifts are done with a wrap or towel. They help to relax an anxious dog, and where a dog is picky or off his food can encourage him to eat. Start the lifts behind the elbows. Holding the ends of the wrap, gently lift for a count of four, hold for another four, then slowly release for a count of eight: the release is the important part of the exercise.

Zigzags can relieve tension, tight muscles or fatigue. Standing to the side of the dog, rest your fingers on his shoulders and lightly zigzag your hand along his back, spreading your fingers as you move your hand away and drawing them together as your hand moves back.

Tail Work reduces tension in the back and hindquarters. Support the tail lightly with one hand and circle it gently in both directions, within a range of motion that is comfortable for the dog. If the dog is nervous about this, cup your hand over the top of the tail and use Python Lifts down the tail and hindquarters.

Python Lifts can be done anywhere on the body. To release tension in the neck, for example, place the whole hand lightly on the neck and gently slide the skin and muscle towards the back of the skull; pause for a few seconds then slowly return to the starting point. Move your hand down slightly and repeat the lift.

Leg Circles help to loosen stiff joints and increase circulation in the limbs and paws. Support the leg without gripping it and circle carefully in both directions, making small circles over the place the paw would be if it were on the ground.

Rock the withers by placing one hand, palm down, over the withers and gently send them away from you, pause for a moment then slowly bring them towards you; repeat a few times.

Tiger is similar to the Clouded Leopard TTouch but with the fingers spread apart so that you are making individual mini circles with your finger tips whilst your thumb rests gently on your dog for support

Snail's Tail is the same as the Clouded Leopard TTouch but with a small addition which is fantastic for reducing discomfort or concern. After completing the one and a quarter circle, maintain the contact and move the skin backwards for a quarter of a circle (anticlockwise if you were doing the TTouch in a clockwise direction)

Springbok requires you to use your fingers to make a light, gentle plucking movement on your dog. Fast Springboks can be useful for energising a sluggish dog whilst slow Springboks can be brilliant for calming an excitable dog. This TTouch can also be used to access ticklish areas on the body. Make sure that you do not pinch your dog or pull his hair if he is long coated.

Troika is used for dogs that may be worried about the sensation of the skin moving. The fingers slide gently over the body in a circular movement rather than actually moving the skin as with the other circular TTouches.

Tarantula involves placing your hands on your dogs back or neck with your thumbs touching and 'walking' your fingers up towards the head, going against the lie of the coat. Your thumbs will form the 'plough' and your fingers will be the spider! You can also do this TTouch with one hand, up legs or anywhere in fact, to improve connection and to release tension.

Turtle is one TTouch where we use both hands at the same time and can be done on the body or down the legs. Lay your hands gently on your dog and move the skin slowly in circles with one hand leading and the other following. Imagine that you are rolling a ball between your two hands so that the movement flows and to ensure that your hands are not completely mirroring each other.

Related ideas...   5   6   10

TTouch ground work and equipment

TTouch practitioners combine body work with ground work exercises using a range of equipment such as poles and boards, as well as body-wraps and harnesses. The slow movements help dogs to settle, improve focus, increase flexibility and improve gait. Physical and emotional balance are linked, so by improving your dog's coordination in this way you can help him to overcome a variety of problems.

You can set up a fun ground work course at home in your yard or garden. There's no need to buy specific equipment, as you can make your own labyrinth, walk-over poles and fan from lengths of water pipes, broom handles or guttering; plastic water bottles filled with sand make excellent weave cones, and crushed drinks cans make great supports for the walk-over poles. Different surfaces can be made from car mats, plastic trays, doormats, carpet samples and so on.

Labyrinth requires a dog to negotiate a simple course made from six poles laid out on the ground as shown. This exercise helps to improve coordination and self-control, and can have a calming effect on even the most boisterous of dogs. You can use poles, guttering, broom handles or even lengths of rope.

Teeter totter is a low-level seesaw with a plywood platform, covered in mats to prevent the dog from slipping, and rockers made from small arc-shaped pieces of ply. Teaching a dog to walk over a moving surface improves confidence, balance, coordination and trust.

Raised board is a flat, level board raised on a wooden base, with ramps or steps leading to the top. Some nervous dogs find it hard to leave the ground on cue. If the dog is too worried about the raised board, build his confidence by working over boards laid flat on the ground to begin with. This simple exercise helps to improve confidence, self-control and physical balance.

Fan consists of six poles arranged in a fan shape – the end where they meet can be raised on a small block to increase the difficulty of the exercise. Walking over the poles improves flexibility through the neck, back and ribs, which is useful for dogs that are stiff and/or tense through the top line, and also helps to improve paw/eye coordination.

Raised poles consists of several low-level poles raised on blocks at both ends, which encourage the dog to lower his neck and soften his back when walking over them. This releases tension and can be a vital stepping-stone for dogs that are reactive or have a high chase drive.

Uneven poles is similar to the raised poles, but with alternate ends of the poles raised. This exercise improves coordination and helps dogs to focus and be more thoughtful in their action.

Pick up sticks requires you to lay out an assortment of objects in a random pattern for the dog to step through: they could be poles, old bicycle tyres, hula-hoops, pool noodles, broom handles, lengths of old rope or you can use a short length of wooden ladder, as we have done here.This exercise improves paw/eye coordination and focus.

Different surfaces is a great starting point for dogs that leap about or are nervous of different floor surfaces, because it really encourages them to become more thoughtful and move beyond their instinctive responses. Set up a pattern of textured surfaces such as rubber car mats, carpet samples, lengths of wood and plastic mats. You can also fill some cheap plastic trays with materials such as soil, rubber granules or sand – be creative!

Working between barriers can help teach confidence to a clingy dog and is also useful for dogs that jump up at their handler as they walk. You do not need two people for this exercise but it can be helpful to give the dog a little extra support.

Sliding line is a good leading technique that teaches confidence and self-control; it's a brilliant way to help dogs overcome issues such as pulling, chasing and spinning. Thread a length of climbing rope through the back rings of a step-in or TTouch harness, hold one end of the rope and give the other end to your helper. Do not start creeping up the line towards your friend, or your dog will end up as the filling in a human sandwich.

Balance-lead plus is a neat extension of the balance-lead where the lead is taken behind the offside shoulder, between the front legs, across the chest and up through the collar. This stops it rising up to the base of the neck.

Balance-lead is a quick way to help reduce pulling or teach calm behaviour when watching an exciting activity. You will need a long training lead. Hold the lead near the collar in your near hand and loop the length around the dog's chest, holding the end of the lead in the other hand. Give him an 'ask and release' signal by pulling up and back, without jerking, to make him shift his weight back on to all four feet, then releasing the tension. This will slow him down and improve his balance.

Homing pigeon involves leading a dog between two people and is an excellent way to teach him to be led and handled from both sides (many dogs are one-sided), to accept a new person and to improve balance and self-control. Attach each lead to a different point of contact but do not use two separate collars: if you do you may garrotte your dog!

Face-wrap is a mini-version of the body-wrap that is used around the dog's head to improve concentration and reduce excessive vocalization. You can make your own from soft elastic or purchase the ready-made TTouch calming band.

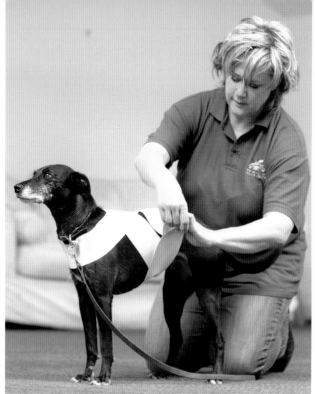

Body-wrap is a length of stretchy bandage that can be put on dogs in a variety of ways to give confidence and help them settle and focus. There should be plenty of give in the wrap, so be careful that you do not put it on too tightly; avoid using crêpe bandages as they will curl up and cause the dog discomfort.

Double diamond helps you to contain and steer the rear end of the dog. Fold a soft double-clipped lead in half and hold the centre. Pass one end diagonally under the dog's tummy and clip it to the side ring of the harness. Repeat with the other end in the opposite direction so that the lead crosses underneath. Knot it loosely over the dog's back so it does not over-tighten and hold the lead by the loop above the knot.

Head-wrap can be introduced as a halfway step for dogs that are worried by the face-wrap. This fancy application of the elastic produces some positive results.

Wands, fakes hands and paintbrushes are used to initiate contact with nervous and defensive dogs. They enable us to start touching the dog without threatening them by being too close and also change a dog's expectation of what contact on their body may mean.

Related ideas…　　9　　11　　14　　15　　16

Work with rewards

Rewards let your dog know that he is doing the right thing, and he will naturally repeat a behaviour that has resulted in a reward. Make sure that you reward *every* instance of good behaviour, no matter how small, because if it goes unrewarded it will rapidly diminish. If your dog is getting things right and you are happy with him, let him know and this will motivate him to please you.

11

There are four main types of reward: food, toys, physical contact and verbal praise. When using reward-based, motivational training you must know what your dog finds pleasurable, and to what degree. Try to use the lowest value rewards in each category when there is little or no distraction, and increase the value when more exciting things have grabbed his interest. Don't just rely on food or toys: physical contact and praise are valuable tools that you always have at your disposal.

Food

Food rewards establish behaviour quickly, but tidbits do not have to be large; in fact dogs seem to work harder if they are broken into very small amounts. Think about which foods he loves the most so that you know which incentives to use in the most testing situations. You can also give your dog a 'jackpot' (several treats one after another) when he gets that light-bulb moment and really understands what you are asking him to do.

Toys

If your dog is motivated by toys and the excitement of a game, find out which articles are 'must haves' for him – they might not be the fancy, store-bought ones *you* like.

Physical contact

Most dogs love contact from their owner: a gentle pat, a few TTouch circles, a scratch behind the ears or at the base of the tail can be very rewarding to your dog.

Verbal praise

Never underestimate the power of the spoken word! You only have to look at your dog and say 'Good boy' in a pleasant tone to realize how important praise is to him. Even shy dogs that are shut down and initially unresponsive to other rewards will usually manage a brief tail wag on hearing praise and kind words.

Teaching a new behaviour

Food is usually the most effective reward in training a new behaviour. Initially, reward your dog each time he responds in an appropriate way, using the same type and amount of reward so that he really understands what you are teaching him. Once he cottons on to the exercise, vary the type, value and timing of the reward: if it becomes too predictable, he may lose interest.

What your dog finds rewarding

Rewards are not just cuddles, games, toys and tidbits. They are anything that your dog finds rewarding such as the chance to sniff the ground when out on the lead. They also include your attention (even if it is just a look) or the feeling he gets after tail chasing and so on. It is important that you understand that a human might view some of these 'rewards' as both unpleasant and unrewarding, but you need to look at the world through the eyes of your furry friend. If your dog keeps repeating a behaviour that you do not like, really think about why he may be motivated to continue to respond in the way that he does.

TIP

If your dog demands a reward by barking or pushing and grabbing at it, quietly end the exercise. Rewards are only really effective when controlled and are certainly not available on demand.

Cookie loves playing with empty drink bottles; they are light and can be stuffed with treats.

Related ideas...   1   4   8   39

12 Teach your dog to look at you

It is surprising how many dogs lack focus and do not make eye contact with their owner. Some are threatened by it, some are easily distracted and others may have learnt to watch the hand that dispenses treats. The clicker is an excellent way to teach your dog to look you in the eye, and TTouch work can also help him to gain confidence and improve his focus.

Skipper responded well to clicker training but he started watching the hand that was dispensing the treats. Sarah used the clicker to teach him to make eye contact with her.

If you and your dog have already used a clicker it will be easier to teach him to look at you because he will already understand what the clicker means. If you have not yet done any clicker training you can still try this exercise, as it is a good way to introduce your dog to the device.

Call your dog and when he comes to you click and give him a treat. Move from your original spot and call your dog again. Repeat this a few times so that your dog really understands what the clicker means. Once he consistently comes when called, you can teach him to look at you.

Call your dog and when he comes, wait for a moment before you click. He may look at you wondering if you have forgotten the reward; the moment he glances at your face, click and throw him a treat.

If he is fixated on your hand, call his name and click and treat the moment he glances up at you. You can point at your eye with your index finger and when the dog looks at your finger, click and treat so that he gets the idea that looking at your face earns him the reward.

Repeat the exercise several times during the day and once your dog is confidently looking at you, add a verbal cue such as 'look'. You can then phase out the clicker. Keep the sessions short – if he loses interest do some of the TTouches listed, play a game and make the next session even shorter. Putting a body-wrap or T-shirt on him may help if he loses focus quickly.

TTouches

- Ear Slides
- Llama TTouch over the whole body
- Chimp TTouch around the muzzle
- Python Lifts down the legs
- Clouded Leopard TTouches over the whole body
- Raccoon TTouches around the back of the skull

TIP

Researchers at Lincoln University have found that the majority of dogs show a 'left gaze bias'. That means they look at the right side of the human face, so it is going to be easier for your dog if you teach him to look at your right eye.

USEFUL GROUND WORK EXERCISES

Different surfaces

Raised poles

Labyrinth

If you carry treats in your pocket, your dog will learn to watch your hand and not your face. It's more effective to keep the treats in a bag placed on a nearby table for this exercise.

Related ideas...   8   81   85   86

Muzzle-train your dog

This exercise is so important for dogs that have issues with other dogs, people and livestock or wildlife. It is also useful for dogs that are overly mouthy when interacting with other dogs, as this may frighten another dog and escalate reactive behaviours in both animals.

Teaching your dog to wear a muzzle is not cruel, provided it is introduced in a way that is kind and fun and the muzzle fits appropriately. If your dog has any of the issues above he will have more freedom and you will stay more relaxed (which in turn will help your dog) if he is wearing a muzzle.

Preparatory work

If your dog is reluctant to be handled around the head, start by using TTouches on all the areas that will be in contact with the muzzle. If he really does not like the muzzle spend more time using the TTouches and use an elastic face-wrap and/or calming band (see page 26) to accustom him to wearing something on his head. If it continues to be an issue take him to the vet for a health check as he may have problems with his ears, teeth or neck.

Targeting the muzzle

Place the muzzle on the floor and throw a treat near it. When the dog walks (or runs!) towards the muzzle, click once and let him pick up the treat. Repeat this exercise: when he is confidently moving towards the muzzle, stop placing a treat near it. Instead, wait to see if he walks or even glances towards it, looking for the treat – the moment he does, mark the behaviour by clicking and throwing him a treat.

Once the connection between the muzzle and the click and treat is established, he should start moving directly towards it and you can delay the click a little so that he moves even closer. When he is moving straight to the muzzle, withhold the click for a moment. He may touch the muzzle with his paw, or push it with his nose. Mark any behaviour that involves him connecting with the muzzle. If he is pushing it with a paw, mark this for a few repetitions so that he understands that you want him to touch the muzzle, then withhold the click. He should start experimenting and may try pushing or touching it with his nose. Mark any move that he makes towards the muzzle with his nose.

Pick up the muzzle and, when he touches it, click and drop a treat on the floor. Shape the behaviour further by using the clicker to mark any move towards putting his snout into the muzzle, remembering to mark all of the small steps, especially in the early stages.

The next step is to shape the behaviour so that your dog pops his nose just inside the muzzle. Continue with the clicker and the treats until he has learnt to put his whole nose inside the muzzle and keep it there while you hold it in place. When he is happy to have the muzzle on his snout, gently take the straps around his head and hold them in place for a few seconds. Continue until you can buckle the muzzle and post some yummy treats through it into your dog's mouth.

TTouches

- Chimp TTouch around either side of the jaw
- Ear Slides
- Raccoon TTouches around the back of the skull
- Clouded Leopard TTouches around the head and down either side of the neck

Teaching your dog to target the muzzle will give him a pleasant association with this vital piece of equipment.

Related ideas... 14 91

14 Teach your dog to accept a collar

Some dogs dislike having their collar put on or touched. This is generally because they either have a negative association with the collar, or because it is a new experience for them. This reluctance has nothing to do with dominance, and forcing the collar on a dog will only escalate his concerns.

Use TTouches around the pelvis, ears (if he's happy to have them touched) and collar area to help reduce any tension in the neck and back. Try making a harness out of rope, or working with a TTouch harness if you want to take him out, as he may well resist a harness that slips over his head. Avoid any collar that tightens around the neck and invest in a flat collar. It can also be a good idea to teach him to hand target and follow, as in *100 Ways to Train the Perfect Dog*. You can also build up his trust through games and free ground work in your home.

Teach him to target the collar when it is lying on the ground. Continue to shape this exercise, as explained in Way 13, until he is confident to target the collar while it is in your hand and is targeting on a verbal cue.

The half body-wrap (see page 26) can be an invaluable tool to help him change his expectation of having something around his neck. As the body-wrap is stretchy it will move with him. Lay the collar on his back while he is wearing his wrap and click and treat all his quiet behaviours. If he is still calm and happy to stay next to you, squeeze some doggy paté onto a fridge door and quietly pop the collar loosely around his neck. Play a game and encourage him to move around while he is wearing the collar before you attach a lead.

Damage in the neck will usually result in unlevel ears. Ask your vet for a through health check and request a referral to a canine osteopath or a physical therapist if your dog's ears are unlevel.

Related ideas...   13   16   74   75

15 Problems with a harness

Dogs that cannot tolerate a harness may have concerns with containment or have physical issues including ear, neck, shoulders, ribs and or/back problems. Invest in a TTouch harness, which can be unclipped in four places: this enables you to put it on your dog without pulling it over his head or picking up his legs.

TTouches

- Leg Circles

- Shoulder Lifts with wraps

- Python Lifts down the shoulders, along the back and down the front limbs

- Turtle TTouches on the shoulders and through the ribs

- Raccoon TTouches between and around the shoulder blades

Start by teaching the dog to wear a half-wrap, following the exercise on page 75. The body-wrap will stretch as he breathes and moves and should reduce any panic he may have felt at wearing a harness. Use TTouches around your dog's body to accustom him to contact in the areas that will be touched by the harness. Avoid rushing, and try to do a little bit every day.

Oscar can be defensive when his harness is put on, particularly if he is already aroused. His owner rewards his calm behaviour as he is introduced to the wrap.

Related ideas...   14   16   54

Accepting the lead

The principles for this exercise and the reasons that dogs become overly excited or worried by the lead are usually the same as problems with the collar. The dog may also have learnt to grab and leap about the moment the lead appears because he associates the lead with fun and games. He may even have been hit with a lead at some point in his life or encouraged to rag on it.

Changing his expectation of what the lead means is a vital step to helping him stay calm and settled when the lead is being attached. Teaching the 'off' or 'leave' cue, as shown in *100 Ways to Train the Perfect Dog,* is also important.

You can teach him to target the lead on cue so that you shape a different behaviour. This will be easier than simply asking him to stay still. It is also important to handle the lead so that you remove some of the triggers for excitable or worried behaviour.

Make or buy a light short line (no more than 6 inches long, or shorter if your dog is little or very young) with a small clip so that you can work with something that does not look or feel like a regular lead. Work through the steps in Way 14 if he is worried about you touching his collar. Click and treat to mark quiet and calm behaviours as you touch his collar, but make sure that you do not click right next to his ears.

Teach him to carry the short length of lead at home by attaching it and letting it hang while you play a quiet game with him, such as searching for food. Take it off and repeat the exercise on and off over a period of days so that he does not merely associate the lead with an outside activity.

You can also try threading some thin rope through the collar; if he panics you can pull the rope from the collar without having to get too close. Loosely hold the rope and use the hand-touch and follow exercise to teach him to walk forward.

Lead grabbing

If he grabs the lead and starts to rag, try having two leads on your dog. Each time he grabs one lead quietly release it and pick up the other lead in a smooth calm manner. The moment he drops the lead in his mouth, click and give him a treat. You may have to repeat this several times in order to change his behaviour. Shouting at him, trying to pull the lead out of his mouth, or grabbing the leads yourself will probably make him more excited.

Dexie cannot tolerate a lead on his collar and when excited grabs the lead and pulls.

Teaching Dexie to carry a toy, ground work and body work all combine with clicker training to calm his behaviour and to start the steps towards walking calmly and in balance on the lead.

USEFUL GROUND WORK EXERCISES

Sliding line

Labyrinth

Weave cones

TTouches

• *Ear Slides*

• *Stroking with the wand*

• *Leg Circles, if it is safe to do so*

• *Belly Lifts*

• *Mouth Work*

Related ideas...   14   48

17 Submissive urination

As with many unwanted behaviours there can be many causes behind this problem. It can be linked to young, excitable dogs and those who are nervous around people. Female dogs with docked tails are more likely to suffer from urinary incontinence than those with their tails intact, or there could be an underlying medical condition.

Timid dogs can suffer from submissive urination; TTouches around the hindquarters and a quiet calm greeting are key to helping dogs develop confidence.

Think if your dog has received any treatment recently, such as spaying, or if anything else has changed in your dog's routine or diet. If there is something in the past that has caused this behaviour, you may never get to the bottom of it. He may have been told off or smacked for jumping up to greet visitors or returning family members; aversive techniques could have been used in training; he might have been confused by conflicting messages in the home; he could have been living in a state of duress, or lacked early socialisation and is timid. It is worth remembering that many young dogs mature out of the problem.

Teach a calm greeting

Over fussing your dog and overexcitement can be a trigger, so stay calm and neutral when you greet him. If he does urinate do not make a fuss, and quietly clean it up when he is settled.

It may sound obvious, but make sure that your dog has had the opportunity to relieve himself outside – a full bladder will naturally add to the likelihood of this happening.

Teach him an alternative greeting behaviour as shown in *100 Ways to Train the Perfect Dog*. Slip your thumb into his collar if he is desperate for your attention and gently and slowly stroke his ears, or start with a few circular TTouches to help him settle and to give him the attention he wants without over stimulating him. Ensure that every family member and visitors use the same techniques.

Treats

It can be a good idea to keep a treat pot near the point of entry so that your visitors or family members can give him a treat when he greets them calmly. Or, try scattering a few treats for him on the floor away from you so that he has something else to focus on. If this makes the situation worse or he does not want to eat them, stick to the calm greeting mentioned above.

TTouch work around the head can also be useful for calming excitable and nervous behaviour.

TTouches

- *TTouches around the hindquarters*
- *Slow stroking with the back of the hand*
- *Ear slides*
- *Raccoon TTouches down either side of the spine and around the base of the tail*

USEFUL GROUND WORK EXERCISES

Different surfaces

Raised board

Labyrinth

Related ideas...   18   58

Housetraining

Timing and patience is everything with housetraining and diligence is the key. Dogs generally need to relieve themselves on waking, after exertion, when excited, or after a meal. Teaching your dog to go on cue is also a useful tool to help you overcome accidents in the house.

TTouches

- Clouded Leopard around the hindquarters
- Ear Slides
- Mouth Work
- TTouches along the back

Housetraining problems can be the fault of the owner unless there are underlying medical problems. If your dog has spent a long time in a shelter or lived outside, this vital part of his education was probably overlooked. The introduction of an invisible fence can create problems for dogs, because they may have received a shock as they were squatting and now associate the act of urination in the garden with the pain.

Whatever the reason, if your dog does go in the house it is vital that you stay calm and quietly pick up any mess without worrying him. Use a pet-safe cleaning product that removes stains and odour. Do not use bleach or other chemical products as these can actually encourage the dog to urinate more. Punishing him, rubbing his nose in it or shouting at him for making a mistake will not help him learn.

How to avoid mishaps

When you're indoors, keep him in an area where you can monitor him. Watch out for signs that he may want to go, such as circling and sniffing, and walk him quietly outside. Don't shut him in for long periods, and take him out to the garden when he wakes, after a game and after eating.

Make sure that he is actually confident in the yard or garden by playing games and giving him treats; if he is worried by the great outdoors he will not want to interact with you. If he is concerned, use a half-wrap or doggy T-shirt and gradually build his confidence by teaching him some simple games, such as searching for toys and treats. You can

If your dog is young or easily distracted he may need to be walked quietly on the lead after an exciting game, otherwise he may run straight indoors and relieve himself on your carpet.

also set up some simple ground work exercises to help him develop greater confidence.

Stay with him every time you want him to toilet outside so that you can reinforce the appropriate actions with treats and verbal praise, and so help him to learn. You should be aware that some dogs do not like to even urinate in their own back garden, so give him plenty of short walks away from the property. As your dog is performing you can start saying the word 'potty' or 'pee' so that he eventually learns to urinate on cue. You can then give him the cue to relieve himself on your own land.

If your garden is unlit at night, install an outdoor light so that he can see in the dark. Some dogs may be reluctant to squat in a vulnerable position after dusk.

Dogs will often urinate in the rooms that the family use less frequently. Spend time reading or eating in rooms that you rarely use to help overcome this problem.

Different surfaces

Some dogs do not like to urinate on paving slabs or concrete, so you may need to invest in a few rolls of turf initially, as walking on grass (and rugs and carpets!) can trigger the urge to pee. Alternatively you could try filling an old low-sided sand box with soil. Once he has marked an area he is more likely to learn that this is the area that you would like him to use. Try borrowing a friendly dog that will obligingly mark your garden. This may encourage your dog to follow suit and you can back this up with some treats.

USEFUL GROUND WORK EXERCISES

Raised board

Labyrinth

Related ideas... 17   36

Noise sensitivity and noise phobia

Dogs have acute hearing and some breeds are more sensitive to noise than others. Some dogs, such as the Border Collie, have been selectively bred to be highly responsive to sound. Noise sensitivity, fear and phobia seem to be an increasingly common problem and one that can have an extremely distressing and detrimental effect on both the dog and his owner.

Megan is typical of dogs that are timid and worried by noise – she is tense through her hindquarters and around the base of her tail. Working on this area helps to release the tension and improves the circulation, improving her posture and her associated behaviour.

Most dogs that display a fear of loud noises may not only be affected by the more obvious noises such as thunder and fireworks, but may be sensitive to other noises such as drawers or doors shutting, the television, clattering pots and pans, telephones, hot air balloons, air brakes on passing traffic and even sizzling onions on the stove. Noise sensitivity may stem from a lack of socialisation as a young puppy, or the dog may have learned a negative association with specific sounds. This sensitivity may have been apparent early on in the dog's life but may have gone unnoticed; he may have simply walked out of the kitchen when he heard the pan drawer opening, or become overly aroused and therefore appear as though he was just having a game when he heard the phone ringing.

Slight noise sensitivity in itself does not necessarily present a huge problem to the dog or his owner, and some dogs are naturally more emotional, and thus more affected by noise

than others. However, when the sensitivity has developed to such a stage that it has become a fear or phobia, life can be miserable for all concerned – particularly during storms, the hunting season and/or around festivities that use fireworks as part of the celebrations. It is vital on occasions like this that he is kept inside, as many a dog has bolted from the garden during a storm or firework display.

Dealing with fireworks

Close the curtains so that the dog cannot see any accompanying flashes of light, and turn on the radio or play a CD that is calming and consistent. Music that has long quiet gaps for example, or 'The Charge of the Light Brigade' is probably not the most appropriate choice.

Set up somewhere for your dog to den. This may be an indoor kennel or an indoor crate, but if you do use a crate that is made of bars as opposed to something solid, cover the crate with a large blanket. Leave the door open so that your dog is free to come and go as he pleases; if he feels trapped because he has been shut in he will panic more. You also need to ensure that his indoor kennel or bed is not in a place where the sound will reverberate more, such as an alcove.

TTouch

The majority of dogs that are noise phobic are also sensitive to contact around the hindquarters, feet and ears. They may have habitually cold ear tips, cold feet and cold or cooler patches over the hind quarters. The base of the dog's tail may be tight and there will usually be tension in the lower back.

The good news is that TTouch can help to change the habitual posture of the dog, increase circulation to the cold extremities and release tension through the back and hindquarters, thus altering the dog's responses to noise. It has helped countless dogs of all ages worldwide.

TTouches

- *Gentle Chimp or Llama TTouches around the muzzle*
- *Clouded Leopard TTouches around the head and base of the ears*
- *Lying Leopard TTouches around the chest and down the shoulders*
- *Clouded Leopard TTouches either side of the breast bone*
- *TTouches around the hindquarters*
- *Gentle Tail Lifts*
- *Python Lifts down the front and hind legs including inside the hind leg*

While dog appeasing pheromone (DAP) diffusers may be helpful in settling your dog, *your* actions will play a huge role in how your dog responds to noise. Dogs look to those around them for guidance when they are feeling unsure, so you need to stay calm and ensure that you do not escalate your dog's anxiety by displaying concern or panicking yourself.

Of course we understand how distressing it can be to see a dog that is frantic with worry, particularly if the dog is doing the wall of death around the living room, salivating and panting heavily, but the more neutral you can stay about the noise, the calmer your dog will be. By all means try to encourage your dog to play a game, but don't try to teach him something new or act out of character by suddenly running wildly around the room trying to entertain your dog in a bid to take his mind off the problem. And we hope that it goes without saying that a dog must never ever be told off for displaying fear.

We have noticed a link between noise phobia and ill health in some of our case histories, so the first step may be to rule out any possible medical cause by asking your vet to give your dog a thorough health check particularly if you have noticed a sudden change in your dog's responses to noise. Back and hip problems, ear infections and the onset of arthritis are just some of the conditions that have been found in dogs that are noise sensitive.

The body-wrap is one of the best TTouch discoveries on the planet! The feeling of the wrap on the body seems to diffuse the focus from the sound and enables the dog to settle and stay calm.

TIP

A body-wrap or T-shirt can be used at home, in the car or when out and about. You can also use a human T-shirt: put it on with the label on top of the dog's shoulders and tie the excess material in a knot on top of the dog's back.

AT HOME

Case History

TARA

Ever since Shona adopted Tara from a shelter as a puppy she has been a slightly nervous dog. As the years have gone on Tara has grown in confidence and, with some careful care and training, has developed into one of the loveliest little dogs you could ever meet. With those she knows she is outgoing, clever and easily trained, but still has a hint of nervousness around strangers, both human and canine. Fireworks remain Tara's biggest fear. Her extreme reactions have ranged from shaking uncontrollably, panting heavily, 'digging' carpets and sofas, hiding in the divan drawer under the bed and once even climbing into the washing machine in an attempt to flee the terror that surrounded her. The stress that Tara endured was heartbreaking and upsetting for her owners to witness, so they got in touch with Sarah Fisher. Sarah instantly recognized some signs in Tara that she commonly finds in noise sensitive dogs; signs that Shona had noticed but didn't realize were connected to her concerns. Tara had never liked her paws being touched nor did she like being stroked on her hindquarters. Sarah also explained that Tara's owners needed to try to keep themselves calm – they were overreacting to the sound of fireworks in anticipation of Tara's fearful responses, and this was sending her into even more of a panic.

Since the session everything that Sarah talked about has helped, but the most effective way of easing Tara's stress levels has been the TTouch techniques. This gentle method of body work visibly reduces Tara's symptoms, and has also helped her owners to stay calm, providing them with something to think about rather than merely focusing on the fireworks. Sarah introduced Tara to the body-wrap, which has helped to settle her, and she also showed the owners a doggy T-shirt that could be used instead of the wrap. Tara and her owners now use TTouch very successfully and enjoy every minute of it. They never leave home without Tara's T-shirt and it is a quick and easy method of reducing her stress level, as is keeping up with the TTouch body work. Tara has managed to get through various scary times, like Christmas, New Year and noisy football games using this approach.

Related ideas...

20   34

20 Separation anxiety

Dogs by nature are very sociable animals and enjoy the company of people and/or other dogs. Separation anxiety can also be linked to noise sensitivity or boredom and it is unfair to expect a dog to tolerate long periods of loneliness, particularly if he lacks confidence.

Cookie Dough Dynamo was handed into Battersea Dogs and Cats Home when she was just 16 weeks old, but she had already developed many unwanted behaviours. She was fostered by Sarah, and we had to think of every possible way to keep this clever puppy entertained. She has now matured into a wonderful companion and friend.

This is a very distressing behaviour for both the dog and the owner. Many dogs are handed into shelters because they cannot cope when left alone, and some are sadly put to sleep because they cannot overcome this problem. For other dogs it may be the act of the person actually coming home that triggers the distress, as they may have been beaten for making a mess in the house or for being destructive. Some people deliberately encourage their dog to be clingy to fulfil their own needs, without realising the full impact this will have on their dog long-term. When they cannot cope with the escalating problem the dog often ends up at a shelter.

TTouch ground work and body work

Most dogs that have separation issues walk closely next to their owner when on the lead, and are usually very fearful if another person tries to walk them away from the person they rely on for their security. Ground work can form an important part of the rehabilitation process, as well as the exercise in *100 Ways to Train the Perfect Dog* to address this.

Invest in a doggy T-shirt that will give your dog a sense of security and give him some physical contact. Avoid fussing him every time he comes to you for attention. We are not advocating that you ignore your dog but over fussing a nervous or timid dog can encourage him to become totally dependent on you. Stay neutral and carry on doing what ever you were doing if he becomes demanding, but remember to set aside time for some relaxing TTouch sessions.

Introduce him to other people so that his whole world does not revolve around you. Ask them to feed him and play with him. Teach them how to do some body TTouches if he is happy to be handled by another person. Teach him to search for hidden treats and toys so that you are not the only source of comfort and rewards, and to help him learn that good things happen when he is away from your side.

TTouches

- *Either side of head*
- *Mouth Work*
- *Ear Slides*
- *TTouches around the hindquarters and tail*
- *Lifts down legs*
- *Clouded Leopard TTouches over the withers*

Triggers

Make a list of all the triggers that your dog associates with being left alone, such as putting on your shoes, turning off the television, radio or lights, picking up your car keys, putting on your coat and so on. Work through all the triggers without actually leaving the house, and teach him to settle in his bed using the exercise in *100 Ways to Train the Perfect Dog*.

Build slowly and try leaving him for short periods in the garden while you are in the house. Give him plenty of things to entertain him while you're doing this, such as searching for food, and extend this to leaving him for short periods in the house. When we say short we really mean short – ideally he should not be left for more than a few minutes at a time. Stay calm and neutral when you leave or return so that he does not get flooded with attention. If you fuss him he will miss the attention all the more when you go, or have his anxiety reinforced by your own actions when you come home. Give him something that has your scent on, such as an old sweatshirt, so that he feels safe when you leave him.

Above all, be realistic and fair. This is not a problem that will be solved overnight, but with patience, consistency and understanding you can help your dog overcome his fears.

USEFUL GROUND WORK EXERCISES

Homing pigeon

Sliding line

Labyrinth

Leading between barriers

Raised board

Related ideas... 19 21 22 26

Chewing

Boredom and stress are usually the roots of excessive chewing, and if a dog is left alone all day he is quite within his rights to make his own entertainment. Gnawing is a natural behaviour and an important part of his development, and while this behaviour is usually associated with younger dogs or teething puppies, frustration is a common problem for many dogs.

Excessive chewing can be a sign of a super-intelligent dog that is not being motivated appropriately, so it is important to keep him physically and mentally stimulated. Get creative with ground work such as negotiating different surfaces; any exercise that involves slow movement will encourage the dog to settle. A dog that has had a good run and explored new territory is more likely to sleep when left alone – a satisfied dog is a quiet dog.

Provide your dog with plenty of chew toys or chew treats and when you see him select his toy for a good gnaw, praise him. If he starts to chew the table leg, rug or tapestry cushion you just inherited you can then quietly redirect him to a more appropriate article.

Some dogs are naturally more prone to using their mouths than others and need an outlet for these drives. If your dog falls into this category invest in toys that encourage him to use his brain *and* his mouth. The Tug-a-Jug or toys from the Nina Ottosson range (see page 126 for suppliers) are particularly good.

Physical causes

Check that your dog's diet is appropriate, as excessive chewing may indicate that he is missing vital nutrients or has some gut dysfunction. It may also be worth taking him for a full health check as the problem can be linked to pain.

Case History
DENNIS

Dennis the Labrador chewed the kitchen when left alone, even though he lived with another dog. Dennis also had other issues: he was worried about being touched, nervous of the vacuum cleaner, had poor recall and lacked focus when out on a walk. Tina Constance, one of our top practitioners, worked with Dennis when he came to Tilley Farm with his owner Ellen.

When Tina first introduced TTouches, Ellen did not feel that Dennis was enjoying the session. Tina broke the work down into small, simple steps, combining ground work with the TTouches listed. She continued with the body work and ground work during their second session, and Ellen was now totally hooked on TTouch. Dennis stopped destroying the kitchen after the first appointment and continues to improve. Although he still chews the odd thing at times, he can be left at home without giving the kitchen a complete makeover.

Teaching your dog to search for hidden treats and toys is a great distraction for him and keeps his mind and body occupied. Cookie was also taught to enjoy Kongs and balls that dispense treats and was left for short periods that were gradually extended.

TTouches

- *Mouth Work*
- *Ear Slides*
- *Tail Work*
- *Chimp TTouch around the muzzle*
- *Clouded Leopard TTouches around the head and jaw*
- *Zigzags*

Related ideas...   **20**   **22**   **29**   **30**   **43**   **48**

22 Excessive barking

Dogs that bark excessively, whether their owner is with them or not, are usually vocalising due to stress or because they have learned that barking gets attention. Providing adequate mental and physical stimulation is key to reducing anxiety and boredom; there is no escaping the fact that a noisy dog is often a bored dog.

If your dog starts barking when you are with him, stay calm and avoid escalating the situation with your own behaviour, however frustrated you may feel. You should also avoid using anything that squirts or shocks him when he starts barking. You need to get to the root of the problem, not just cover up the behaviour.

If the barking has become a habit and you have really addressed all other management factors, use a face-wrap or calming band. The idea is not to tie the mouth shut but to bring awareness to the barking, and most dogs will settle straight away. Make sure that the wrap is loose and that the dog can pop it off with a paw if necessary. A half body-wrap can also help him feel more confident and more aware of his own body. But don't leave wraps on your dog when he is unattended: they are tools to help you help your dog, not to prevent him from expressing his concerns. Dogs that bark excessively usually carry tension through the head, jaw, neck and back, so using TTouches in these areas will go some way in helping your dog to settle.

Sally is a very vocal dog. She had been in at least two homes before she came to live with Tina.

A simple face-wrap made from soft elastic helps dogs to settle.

USEFUL GROUND WORK EXERCISES

Labyrinth
Fan
Weave cones

TTouches

- Ear Slides
- Raccoon TTouches around the back of the neck
- Lying Leopard TTouches over the top of the head
- Clouded Leopard TTouches either side of the temples and across the forehead
- Tail Slides
- Lying Leopard and Clouded Leopard TTouches all over the body

Lady barks because she finds people worrying and, like most dogs, she wags her tail while barking; cupping her tail gently helps her to calm down. Remember, tail wagging is not always a sign of a happy dog.

Related ideas...   20   67   71

Growling

Growling is a natural response that tells other people and animals that the dog is feeling threatened; it is not a direct challenge for dominance. Telling a dog off for growling may encourage him to dispense with this early warning sign and go straight for a bite next time. It is far better to work with the dog to overcome his fears.

Punishing a dog for growling can increase his concerns by reinforcing the threat he thought you represented. Any attempts to 'dominate' the dog by restraining, pinning down or rolling him over are likely to tip his reaction into an instinctive fight for survival. What a dreadful thing to do when the dog may be trying to tell you that his leg hurts, or that he is frightened of the noisy toddler bearing down on him.

Finding the trigger

If your dog growls when you approach him while he is lying in his bed, he is asking you to leave him alone, perhaps because he is feeling stiff after resting or he feels vulnerable. Children, in particular, need to know that a dog should be left in peace when he is sleeping.

If your dog growls when he is eating, teach him that a person near his bowl is a positive experience by following the exercise to deal with food guarding (see page 40).

Study your dog's coat and posture, and run your flat hand slowly and gently all over his body. You may discover that he growls only when you touch a specific area. Take him for a health check to discover if his growling is due to an underlying medical issue: a flare-up of a chronic ear infection, for instance. Look for small signs of anxiety in your dog such as lip licking, going into freeze, lowering or turning his head and so on to establish at which point your dog actually starts to be concerned.

Use any TTouches or ground work and teach him some useful skills such as 'Hand target' and 'Hand follow' as shown in *100 Ways to Train the Perfect Dog* to develop trust and understanding between you and to change his expectation of what human interaction may mean.

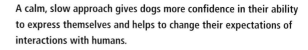

Case History
RASCAL

Sarah was asked to work with a shelter dog labelled as unpredictable because he would sometimes growl and bite when touched but at other times enjoyed the attention. She noticed two small patches of dry, coarse fur on either side of his spine. The dog would growl and bite only when he was touched in these areas, so in fact he was extremely predictable. TTouch helped to reduce his concerns and he made huge steps forward in just one afternoon. Explaining this to the staff meant that they understood the reasons for his behaviour and could continue working with him to help him overcome his problem.

Fred does not always like being touched, though his owner Mina has worked miracles with this little dog. Sarah worked with him using a wand, slowly stroking the floor first to accustom him to it, then gradually touching his paw or shoulder before returning to the floor.

A calm, slow approach gives dogs more confidence in their ability to express themselves and helps to change their expectations of interactions with humans.

Related ideas...   24   27   52

Food guarding

It is a natural instinct for a dog to protect certain resources in his life, and there are a number of reasons why a dog may become stressed around feeding time. Trying to teach the dog a lesson by taking, and then 'possessing', the food bowl of a dog that is already displaying this worrying behaviour is a dangerous practice.

Some unsuspecting dog owners are still taught that a dog that guards his bowl is dominant, and his behaviour is a test to see just how long it will take him to rule the house, his relationship with his owner and, finally, Planet Dog. Even if we don't fully understand the reasons why dogs behave in a particular way, it is important that we work to resolve the issue in a positive and constructive way.

BluBelle is a 10-month-old Neapolitan Mastiff who was found abandoned and emaciated when she was just 20 weeks old. She is still highly protective of her food, despite the hard work of her handler Jaq. The pair joined us at Tilley Farm for a one-to-one session.

Setting up the environment

Arrange two stable, raised surfaces close enough together to ensure that you can move calmly and easily to and fro but with enough space in between to allow the dog to walk to each station in turn and wander around them if he needs to. You will also need two flat plastic plates without rims. Put some rubber matting underneath the plates if you think that they may slide about.

Dogs can set up territories very quickly, so it is a good idea to vary the location of the feeding stations to ensure that your dog doesn't learn to guard a particular area.

Practising the exercise

Stay calm and remember to breathe – jerky, rushed movements will trigger the dog to become aroused. Put a small amount of food on one plate and allow the dog to eat it, and then repeat with the second plate.

DO NOT ATTEMPT TO LIFT THE PLATES YET!

It is vital that you repeat this until the dog is showing no concern whatsoever and moving happily from one plate to the other. Once the dog is settled with this part of the exercise, begin to lift the plastic plates just off the surface as you put food on them. Monitor the dog's reaction at all times and work at a pace that will help him to stay calm.

Continue to shape the behaviour by practising the exercise until the dog is confident that a human around the food bowl means that food is likely to be added, rather than taken away. Be prepared to go back and repeat a step until your dog is completely happy and performing consistently.

Once you are completely happy you can start placing the dishes on the floor, adding food to each dish. If the dog's behaviour deteriorates at this point you have moved too quickly – go back to a stage where the dog remained calm.

While BluBelle is eating from the first plate, Jaq loads the second. The food is raised up from the floor to enable BluBelle to see around her. She has a smaller area to worry about and can eat in a more relaxed posture.

The first time Jaq goes to lift the plate BluBelle's posture changes from relaxed to defensive and challenging, as she senses the threat.

TIP

It has been proved that the majority of aggressive or reactive behaviours are a result of a dog expressing a natural response to fear, confusion, frustration or physical pain.

TTouch

TTouch can be a valuable step in the dog's rehabilitation. Dogs that have defensive behaviours may be tense through the lower back and may dislike contact around their mouth. You can use the TTouch body work exercises (see pages 24–25) to promote a sense of relaxation and wellbeing and to help develop the bond between you. Use the TTouch body work exercises before you start the feeding exercise but obviously not while the food is around or if the dog is already expecting his meal.

TTouches

- *Mouth Work*
- *Ear Slides*
- *Clouded Leopard TTouches around the head, back and hindquarters*
- *Gentle Tail Lifts*
- *Belly Lifts or Lying Leopard*
- *TTouches on the stomach*
- *Light Tarantulas or Lying Leopard TTouches around the ribs*

Ground work

Another way to help dogs to feel more confident in all aspects of their life is through ground work. BluBelle was initially a little worried by the floor surface in the kitchen, so we taught her how to negotiate slippery surfaces outside (see page 99). We also helped her to develop her coordination by working over uneven poles.

Having gone back a step and loaded the plate, while still in situ, Jaq then goes to lift the plate again, keeping it low. BluBelle is perfectly happy with this and feels safe around the plate, her food and Jaq.

Jaq lifts the plate too high and BluBelle becomes more tense – look at the change in her body posture.

After going back a step BluBelle develops more confidence and is relaxed as she watches Jaq adding food to the plate while holding it in her hands.

Related ideas...   1   2   26   41

25 Reactive behaviour

If your dog has serious issues or is showing signs of developing this problem you need to get help on a one to one basis right away. We are not going to take you through the steps in this book because every dog is different and it would be foolhardy for us to suggest that you can address this issue on your own.

We are giving you some pointers and include a case history from one of Sarah's clients to illustrate how powerful TTouch work and a quiet, calm approach can be for dogs that have developed this worrying behaviour.

Identifying the cause

Dogs develop reactive behaviours towards people for a number of reasons, and pain and fear are probably the two most common factors. Some dogs have been deliberately encouraged to behave in such a way and stress can obviously be another major contributory factor. A person in the household may trigger a memory of an unpleasant event in a previous home.

We know of a German Shepherd rescue who had settled well into his new home; a month after the dog was adopted, the male owner went out for a drink. When the man returned home the smell of beer on his breath triggered previously unseen reactive behaviour in the dog, even though the dog had formed a strong bond with his owners. There is always a good reason for unwanted behaviour.

Hip dysplasia is also something to consider and we recommend a thorough veterinary check to rule out any possible underlying medical condition including thyroid imbalance, food allergy or discomfort in the body. If your vet does not understand the link between medical issues and aggression, go elsewhere; and please muzzle train your dog before you ask your vet to handle him. Vets are important and they need their hands!

Educate yourself

Read anything and everything that helps you to recognise the posture and signals that can tell you your dog is under duress.

Make sure that all the family members involved seek help together. It is vital that everyone is in agreement when it comes to helping the dog overcome his concerns, and many dogs are confused by the intentions of well-meaning family members who all expect something different from him. For example, if one person allows him to rest on the sofa and another tries to drag the dog from it is likely that serious problems will develop.

Look for areas of tension in your dog's body and read *Unlock Your Dog's Potential* to see how posture can influence behaviour. Use the TTouch body work and ground work exercises to reduce stress, increase flexibility in the body and to gain a better understanding of your dog's concerns.

Case History

NEMO

'Nemo' came to live with his current owner when he was four years old. He is a male Akita and his history is a little sketchy but his owners do know that he was trained using aversive techniques and was roughly handled. 'Nemo' had lived with his owners for several months before he attacked his male owner. His owner pushed him out of the way when the dog was blocking his path and the dog went for his arm and dragged him to the floor. It took another person to get the dog off his owner and the man was hospitalised for two days. It was a very serious attack and his owner wanted the dog destroyed. Had he done this, no one would have blamed him and it is certainly something that should be considered in situations such as this as he could have easily been killed by his own dog. He is scarred for life.

The dog was not destroyed, however, as the man's partner could not bring herself to kill the dog. And when the man came out of hospital he was faced with a dilemma – what should he do now?

'Nemo' and his owners came to Tilley Farm to work with Sarah and in all honesty Sarah did not want to take them on. However, that first session was to mark the start of an extraordinary journey and the beginning of a wonderful friendship between all those involved. Sarah used the clicker and TTouch to give the owner new tools. She showed the owner where 'Nemo' was carrying tension and ways in which he could rebuild a relationship with his dog.

'Nemo' is now the most loving, gentle giant of a dog. He is a puppy in a four year old's body. He has learnt to play, and is fantastic with other dogs and puppies. His eyes are soft, his movement more fluid and his owner can do anything he wants with his dog – such is the level of trust between them. They have joined the list of Sarah's Favourite Clients and 'Nemo' is able to extend his new found confidence to others. He has many friends and admirers and is a testament to the willingness and openness of his owner who took on board every thing that Sarah said, learnt new skills and found the ability to look at his dog with new eyes.

Related ideas...   23   26   37   79

Guarding the owner

Dogs develop strong bonds with the people who interact with them and, for an insecure dog, the person who walks them, feeds them, plays with them and keeps them company is going to be the whole world. If your dog is guarding you or another member of the household you obviously need to be extremely careful and enlist the help of a trainer who can help you on a one-to-one basis.

Some dogs appear to guard their owner because they are insecure and threatened by another dog or person approaching the one thing that gives the dog a sense of safety. It can also be inadvertently triggered by the owner relying too heavily on their dog for emotional support and encouraging the dog to favour them, or it may be that the dog has had a bad experience in a previous home. It might also be that the dog is uncomfortable through the body, dislikes contact and reacts defensively to anyone approaching him whether the owner is there or not. If the owner is present the dog will run to the person he trusts, and his defensive reactions may be misconstrued as guarding behaviour.

When we are working with a dog with these issues we teach the owner to start working on their dog – it would be stressful for everyone if we launched straight in and started stroking ears and working tails. They usually find their dog is carrying tension in the mouth and through the back and hindquarters. The dog may also have red gums, red eyes and red skin between his pads.

Attention

Learn his body language so that you can monitor his mood, and stress levels. Use a TTouch session to release tension and stress.

Make sure that your dog is getting plenty of attention during the day. If he has been left alone for long periods or if you have been unable to interact with him he is more likely to see your attention as something special that needs to be protected. Teach him that fun *can* be had with you but not always right on top of you. If it is safe to do so, start involving other people in the day-to-day care of your dog so that he learns you are not the sole provider of his daily entertainment. Use the body-wrap to give him more confidence and teach him to target a mat so that you can ask him to go to a mark on cue and to start working away from you.

Ground work

A large majority of dogs that develop guarding problems are working dogs with little or no outlet for their natural instincts. Make sure your dog is getting enough mental and physical stimulation in an appropriate environment. Some dogs are protective of their owners at home but not when out, while for others the big wide world can trigger more insecurity and reactive behaviours.

If your dog has issues when out and about, teach the labyrinth and other ground work exercises, such as raised boards, poles and different surfaces at home.

TTouches

- *Ear Slides*
- *Llama TTouch around the muzzle and all over the body*
- *Chimp TTouch around the muzzle*
- *Troika TTouch all over the body*
- *Clouded Leopard TTouches around the chest and hindquarters*
- *Raccoon TTouches around the back of skull*
- *Clouded Leopard TTouches either side of the head and over the top of the skull*

Lady is muzzled because she has issues with people. She has a positive association with the muzzle and this gives her more freedom and the ability to start working with other people safely. A harness and wand help to keep her calm and in balance as she walks on the lead. Tina begins working with Lady by using the wand to initiate contact and to let Lady know that she is not a threat.

Lady's owner keeps up with the TTouch sessions and as a result she is much calmer and more manageable than when we first met her. There is still a way to go but she is definitely on the right path.

Related ideas...   6   23   25

Coping with children

The noise, movement and excitable games that are a natural part of childhood can be very arousing and worrying for a dog. As much as your dog needs to learn how to behave appropriately around youngsters, your children need to understand how to interact with dogs. It goes without saying that you must supervise all such interactions.

Even the best-mannered child can hurt a dog by mistake, by treading on a paw or tail, and sadly some children may deliberately tease dogs. If you get a rescue dog you cannot be sure what he experienced in his previous home, so be patient with him. Dogs learn by association, and if a dog has had a distressing experience while a child was present he may think that the child was responsible.

Educate the children

Children, like dogs, copy behaviour from their role models, so always treat your dog with respect and encourage any visitors to do the same. Remember, your dog is not viewing the children in the household as 'lower ranking'. Suggesting that a child should become more assertive with a dog is extremely dangerous.

Try to borrow a well-educated dog that is used to children and teach your children to use the back of their hand to initiate contact. Involve them in all aspects of the care, training and management of your dog, so that they can bond and get to know the dog's likes and dislikes. As the dog gains confidence, recruit one of your children to lead him in ground work exercises.

Help the dog relax

If your dog becomes stressed when children are around use the TTouches listed to relax him. When noisy games are taking place or hoards of children descend on your home, find somewhere quiet for your dog to go and chill out.

You may need to seek help on a one-to-one basis if your dog is really concerned by children. If the situation becomes too difficult to manage, you may even need to consider re-homing him. If your dog is concerned by children it is particularly important that you can give the child some valuable information as to how they should behave in the

Gracie the Dalmatian puppy is anxious about Rachel kneeling on the floor.

Marie encourages Harry and Rachel to sit quietly on the couch so that Gracie feels confident enough to approach.

After a few moments Rachel is able to stroke Gracie with the back of her hand while owner Colleen sits close by.

Cuba is a little concerned when meeting younger children.

company of dogs. If movement is the trigger for the behaviour ask the child to stand still with their arms quietly by their side. They need to avoid eye contact with the dog and asking them to look away can help the dog to become more confident. Some dogs are unsettled by a child sitting on the floor and this can also be a trigger for an uninvited game. Asking the child to sit quietly on a chair or sofa is not about upping the child's status. It is about safety and changing the dog's expectation of what the presence of a child may mean.

Anna walks Cuba quietly past the children using the balance leash and a harness to avoid pulling on Cuba's neck which will panic the dog more.

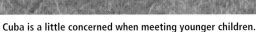
TTouches

- *Ear Slides*
- *Mouth Work*
- *Raccoon TTouches between and around the shoulder blades*
- *Clouded Leopard TTouches and Python Lifts around the hindquarters and down the hind legs*
- *Tail Work*

TIP

The Blue Dog CD-ROM (see page 126) is an excellent interactive tool to teach children how to live safely with a dog. If your family is getting its first dog, you should make sure that you play this on your computer as part of your preparation before he arrives.

Cuba and the children move indoors and Anna rewards Cuba's excellent progress with the clicker and plenty of treats. Rachel and Harry are doing an excellent job of remaining quiet and avoid making eye contact with Cuba.

Related ideas...   23   25   26   45   59

28 Self-mutilation

This problem is usually stress related, and is obviously a more serious condition than repetitive licking or chewing a part of the body. Dietary changes and a full vet check should always be considered.

Self-mutilation can be extremely distressing for both the dog and the owner, and can be linked to pain or discomfort. It doesn't necessarily follow that a dog that chews his tail or his paw has pain in that area; the problem may lie in his back, for example. It may have started with repetitive licking if a thorn or grass seed was buried under the skin and, even if there isn't any visible sign of injury, this must be ruled out as skin can grow over foreign bodies. Over- and under-exercise can also be contributory factors, and dietary allergies may also be to blame. Blocked meridians, damage to soft tissue and/or the skeleton can also trigger self-mutilation, and a referral to a holistic vet who practices acupuncture and/or a physical therapist may be worthwhile.

If a dog was not given an outlet for his natural gnawing instincts he may well have developed this behaviour as a way of dealing with stress. Use Kongs, and/or toys that the dog can chew safely to satisfy his natural urges so that he learns to self calm. Even if the origin of the problem has been resolved, the habit may remain. TTouch work can form a valuable part of the rehabilitation and this includes slow movement through the ground work exercise, in addition to all the body work. Working with your dog using TTouch body work will not only help the dog to relax but may also give you vital information about any tension that he is carrying through his body.

The gorgeous Arnold is now in a home where he is given plenty of attention and lots of positive experiences.

Study your dog's posture and note whether he has unlevel ears and/or whether he is dropped in the pelvis. This will help you to notice improvements in the posture as you work using TTouches and ground work.

Run your hand slowly and gently over his body and note his responses. You might feel hot or cold patches over his head, through the back and over the hind quarters.

Use a harness with a double clipped lead attached to the front ring of the harness and the D ring on the back of the harness – this will help to release any tension in the neck which may exacerbate the disconnection through the body.

Use the TTouches to help improve circulation through the body and to reduce any sensitivity to contact. This will also enable you to help relieve any sensations that the dog may be feeling in his body that trigger the chewing.

Look for early signs of stress and use the TTouches to settle your dog, and a doggy t-shirt to improve his body-awareness.

Case History

ARNOLD

Arnold's previous owners had been out at work all day, and he developed worrying behaviours to cope with being left alone. He would spin around very fast in tight circles and also chew areas of his body; in fact he chewed his genitals and the end of his tail so badly that he had to have them surgically removed. Arnold was adopted by Lyn Raine and the pair came to Tilley Farm for a TTouch session.

When Sarah carried out a flat hand assessment she found that Arnold had ice-cold spots over his hindquarters, which is not uncommon in dogs that chase their tail and/or chew themselves. He was also concerned about hand contact between his hind limbs and around the surgery site, which made it hard for Lyn to keep the wound clean. Arnold had a slight head tilt that may have arisen due to his spinning, since it can cause excessive movement of the cerebrospinal fluid.

Sarah taught Lyn some of the ground work exercises listed to improve Arnold's coordination and trigger feel-good hormones to help him settle more quickly. Within a relatively short period Arnold was calm and focused, and could accept and actually enjoy contact all over his body, including around the surgery site. Arnold still spins, but the frequency is decreasing, and Lyn uses TTouch to help calm him if he starts to become aroused.

TTouches

- *Raccoon TTouches down either side of the spine and around the back of the skull, as well as in the areas that dog is attacking*
- *Ear Slides*
- *Mouth Work*
- *Tail Work*
- *Zigzags*
- *Tiger TTouches*
- *Belly Lifts*

TIP

If you do see your dog chewing a part of his body, stay neutral and walk calmly over to your dog. Use the TTouches on the parts of the body that he is chewing to relieve the sensations.

USEFUL GROUND WORK EXERCISES

Different surfaces

Raised poles

Labyrinth

Related ideas... 9 29 30 31 32

Feet nibbling

29

Diet (including overfeeding and food sensitivity), stress, allergies, low-grade ear infections and poor gut function are just some of the reasons that dogs start nibbling parts of their body to excess.

Stress increases the likelihood of the development of allergies, a major cause of skin irritation. To combat the problem you must eliminate the cause of the dog's stress. It goes without saying that a health check should come first if your dog nibbles himself a lot, and it is well worth asking for a referral to a holistic vet who can explore other options.

TTouch work is useful as it can relieve the itch without causing further damage to the skin. If heat is present in the skin try laying a cool facecloth on the area and use the TTouches on top of the flannel.

TTouches

- *Raccoon TTouches either side*
- *Ear Slides*
- *Clouded Leopard TTouches around the tips of the ears to stimulate the acupuncture point for allergies*
- *Raccoon TTouches on the affected areas*

Ginny had a terrible skin condition when Sarah adopted her. Euthanasia seemed the kindest answer, as Ginny was constantly nibbling her legs and crying and her face was lined with worry. But with appropriate dietary changes and veterinary support she now lives a happy and active life, although some of her hair will never grow back.

Related ideas... 1 28 30 32

30 Tail chewing

If your dog regularly chews his tail you must rule out any possible medical conditions, so your vet should be your first port of call. Tail chewing can also be a sign of frustration or stress, or may indicate that a dog is disconnected from his hindquarters.

TTouches

- *Raccoon TTouches either side of the spine*
- *Raccoon TTouches around the back of the skull and down the neck*
- *Clouded Leopard TTouches either side of the head*
- *Chimp or Llama TTouches around the muzzle*
- *Clouded Leopard and Raccoon TTouches down the tailbone*
- *Ear Slides*

An old injury, irritation, nerve damage or even phantom pain (in the case of dogs with docked tails) can all cause tail chewing. It may also be the sign of an allergy or digestive disturbance, anal gland problems or discomfort in the back and/or pelvic area. The good news is that even if a medical condition is triggering the problem, TTouch can be a fantastic tool for helping to resolve this issue.

TTouch

When Mika first arrived at his new home he had a beautiful tail, but it wasn't long before he started stripping the hair. After a couple of TTouch sessions with us he stopped chewing his tail. Instant success is possible with TTouch as mentioned above, but some dogs may need on-going touchwork, and other management factors may also need addressing.

Habitual pulling on the lead can disconnect the dog from his hindquarters and cause stiffness around the base of the tail, so we used a combination of TTouch body work and ground work to reduce Mika's sensitivity and help him move in balance on the lead. Teaching the dog to walk over raised poles and through the Labyrinth can be an effective part of the rehabilitation process, because improved coordination also improves self-confidence, reducing stress.

If your dog is worried by contact around his hindquarters try putting a half-wrap around his forequarters (see page 75) and work on his shoulders with slow Lying Leopard and/or Clouded Leopard TTouches. Work along his back and switch your hand position so that you can use Raccoon TTouches around the base of his tail.

There is a link between the neck and pelvis. Many dogs with tail issues are tight in the neck and TTouches around the base of the skull can be extremely beneficial, particularly if the dog is worried by contact around the hindquarters.

If your dog is worried about contact on the hindquarters try using zigzags across the back and ribs to access the sensitive area.

USEFUL GROUND WORK EXERCISES

Fan

Raised poles

Labyrinth

Leading from both sides using a harness with a double-ended lead

If your dog clamps his tail use Python Lifts down the tailbone and gently stroke the underside of his tail with your fingers. Once he is happy to have his tail handled, use light Leopard TTouches and/or Raccoon TTouches from the base to the end of the tailbone. Remember to breathe, and keep your hand and fingers relaxed to avoid gripping or pinching the tail.

Related ideas...   28   29   31   32

Repetitive licking

Dogs may lick themselves, humans or even walls to excess in order to relieve tension. Getting to the root of the problem is far kinder than interrupting the behaviour with devices, including bandages, that administer electric shocks.

If your dog has recently started repeatedly licking himself it is wise to get him checked over by a vet. It is possible that he has a food allergy, a foreign body that is irritating him, parasites or a skin infection. While such concerns are being addressed you can help your dog further by using the TTouches to reduce any irritation without causing further damage to the skin.

Excessive licking can also be related to insecurity, boredom and/or stress. Make sure that your dog has enough mental and physical stimulation. If he needs an alternative outlet you can use a Kong stuffed with pâté, which is far more gratifying and appropriate.

Cookie licks people and also licks her lips a lot. Giving her a Kong stuffed with dog pâté gives her a more appropriate outlet for this urge and as a result the behaviour is reducing.

Related ideas... 28 29 30 32

Tail chasing

This can start for the same reasons as for chewing and self mutilation, so read these sections for other tips. Some dogs are also naturally disconnected through their hindquarters, and the sight of their tail out of the corner of the eye can trigger this behaviour. Docking the tail is not the answer.

Carry out a flat hand assessment to ascertain if there are any areas on your dog's body that are sensitive to contact. Study the coat to see if there are any tell-tale signs of an old injury, such as white hairs, missing fur or coarse, rough hair on the tail, through the hindquarters or along the back. Try a half-wrap or T-shirt to increase his body awareness and teach him new skills as shown in *100 Ways to Train the Perfect Dog* to give him alternative outlets for his natural behaviours. TTouches and any slow ground work will help to lower stress levels and release tension, so use them on a regular basis.

If he does start spinning, remain neutral. Laughing, shouting or panicking will teach the dog that this behaviour gains attention. Gently contain him if it is safe to do so using the standing containment exercise as shown in *100 ways to Train the Perfect Dog*. When he has settled give him a Kong or engage him in another quiet activity, but be careful that he does not associate spinning with the arrival of some treats. Keep a diary to see if there is a pattern to the tail chasing. It may be after a walk, at meal times, or it may also be triggered by boredom or anxiety. If a pattern emerges try changing the management of the dog and use TTouch work and clicker training before the spinning starts.

TTouches

- *Ear Slides*
- *Body work all over the body*
- *Tail Work*
- *Clouded Leopard TTouches down the tail*
- *Lifts inside hind legs*

USEFUL GROUND WORK EXERCISES

Labyrinth

Different surfaces

Raised poles

Fan

Sliding line

Double diamond

Related ideas... 28 29 30 31

33 Timidity

Some dogs are naturally more sensitive than others, and this can be linked to build: dogs that are lighter in the bone and have a narrower frame are often more timid than those that are more heavily set. TTouch is excellent in helping with timidity and can have a profound and lasting effect on even the most nervous of dogs.

TTouches

- Llama and Chimp TTouches
- Mouth Work
- Ear Slides
- Gentle Tail Lifts
- Tail Work
- Clouded Leopard TTouches over the whole body
- Python Lifts down the legs
- Raccoon TTouches or a paintbrush on the feet

Timidity is often present in dogs with noise phobia and is usually linked to tension through the hindquarters and around the muzzle. Megan, who is the model for this section, first came to Sarah with her owner Jacqui Ballantyne, as she was nervous of new people, new dogs and worried by noise. Megan was displaying her lack of confidence very clearly. She was lip licking, panting, her ears were down and her tail was clamped underneath her.

Timid dogs may also permanently wag their tail slightly from side to side, which is obviously not the sign of a contented pooch. Some dogs that are timid may be reluctant to sit, have housetraining issues as they may not feel safe outside, or may cower and hide when visitors come to the house. When out and about, they may be unable to urinate and may find it impossible to walk in balance on the lead.

Timid dogs often have cold extremities as circulation to these areas may be reduced as the dog is in the Fight/Flight

Case History

MEGAN

Megan came to Sarah with her owner Jacqui Ballantyne because she was nervous of new people and new dogs, and worried by noise. Megan displayed her lack of confidence very clearly: licking her lips and panting, with her ears down and her tail clamped under her.

Sarah talked Jacqui through the basic TTouches and, once Megan had settled, started working on her. As with many timid dogs, Megan was very tight through the hindquarters so Sarah focused the TTouches in this area. While she was working between the wings of the pelvis Megan suddenly stretched, wagged her tail and bounced towards her companion, Teazel. She then shot around the training barn, play bowing and thoroughly enjoying herself. Her tail remained up for the rest of the session.

Since then, Megan has improved beyond measure. She can now eat and drink when away from home, greet strangers and even initiated a game with a Staffordshire bull terrier she met at an equine event.

Like most nervous dogs Megan was worried about contact on her feet and a soft water-colour brush was the perfect, non-threatening way to introduce TTouches to sensitive paws and help her overcome her fears.

Megan is a very sensitive dog but she is developing new confidence thanks to her dedicated owner.

reflex. If we were worried about going into a new situation we might say that we 'got cold feet' and couldn't participate in the activity/event and the same is true for the timid dog. Most nervous dogs dislike having their feet handled and a soft water-colour brush can be a non-threatening way to introduce TTouches to delicate paws.

TTouch work can have a profound and lasting effect on even the most nervous of dogs, and when we are working with timid dogs we usually teach the owner, or someone that the dog trusts, to start the body work.

USEFUL GROUND WORK EXERCISES

Raised surface

Ladder

Labyrinth

Sliding line

Megan was worried about walking over the raised board but after working with her more confident friend, Teazel, she began to gain more courage.

Related ideas...　　　　　　　　**19**　　**34**　　**50**

Introducing your timid dog

34

If you own a nervous dog you have probably already met that special kind of person who thinks they know your dog better than you – the one who bears down on your quivering dog, hand outstretched, shouting, 'It's fine, I'm really good with dogs.' Just tell them he has a contagious skin disease and they will probably back right away.

It is far more appropriate to let your dog greet people in his own time. Some nervous dogs may well take treats from newcomers or even initially let them touch them, but they are likely to panic when they realize just how close that person is and may bite because they are unable to move away.

Teach your dog to greet you calmly by touching the back of your hand with his nose (as shown in *100 Ways to Train the Perfect Dog*), then involve other people in this exercise. If your dog is happy to approach people and you feel confident that he can be touched by someone else, ask the person to stroke him on the side of the shoulder with the back of their hand. This is a far less threatening approach.

If your dog has serious concerns around new people you will need to enlist the help of someone who can work with you at home to teach him greater confidence.

If your dog is worried, introduce contact with the Llama TTouch and encourage anyone who may be handling your dog to do the same.

Related ideas...　　　　　　　　**33**　　**52**　　**59**

35 Fear of slippery floors

Some dogs are so genuinely concerned about walking across slippery surfaces that they may actually have a panic attack. Dogs that have this concern are usually tight or stiff through the hips and hindquarters and/or have poor balance.

TTouches

- Lifts down legs
- Belly Lifts
- Raccoon TTouches around the neck

It was with great concern that we listened to a trainer advising the owner of a dog who was worried about walking on a highly polished floor that her dog was being dominant. Nothing could be further from the truth.

A health check is important to rule out problems such as arthritis, spondylosis or hip dysplasia. Run your hand over your dog's body to check for cold, hot or sensitive areas, and study his coat – hair will usually stand upright or run in a different direction where there is underlying tension, and there may also be dandruff present. Check that long nails are not affecting his balance and ensure that he does not have lots of hair between his pads, as this will make it harder for him to maintain his grip on a shiny floor.

Use TTouches to help increase flexibility in the back and awareness of the feet, and try a half-wrap or doggy T-shirt to improve coordination. Leg wraps may increase your dog's awareness of his legs and feet. Until he has developed more confidence, lay non-slip mats on shiny floors in your home so that he can move around with ease.

Ground work exercises

Teaching a young dog to negotiate a variety of surfaces is an invaluable part of their education. If you have an older dog you can still help him to feel more stable on a slippery surface by working through these ground work exercises.

Teach the dog to walk across small areas of slippery surfaces such as wooden boards and plastic mats laid out on a surface he is comfortable on, like grass or carpet. Use a wand to stroke his body and legs to improve poor spatial awareness.

USEFUL GROUND WORK EXERCISES

Different surfaces

Raised and uneven poles

Labyrinth

Check your dog for any sensitive areas and look at his posture. Blubelle is growing fast and this can contribute to poor balance.

BluBelle is really enjoying the Python Lifts down her legs, which helped to improve awareness of her limbs.

52

We covered the slippery mats with pieces of carpet and asked BluBelle to walk across them widthways at first, breaking the exercise down into simple steps.

It wasn't long before BluBelle was confident enough to walk directly on to the plastic mats.

We were able to use food as BluBelle was good with treats, and gradually built the exercise up by asking her to walk along a series of mats.

Jacqui also used the uneven poles to help BluBelle's coordination.

Related ideas... 93

36 Coprophagia

Almost every dog will snack on a bit of sheep/horse/fox/any poo on a walk, but coprophagia can be more serious when it comes to a dog eating its own poo or that of another dog. Eating poo is not considered a pleasant habit, particularly if your dog has a tendency to give you big smoochy kisses, but it is important to understand that he is doing it for a reason.

Coprophagia can start because the dog was told off for making a mess in the house and may have been driven to clean up after himself for fear of punishment. He may be eating the faeces because something is lacking in his own diet, or because of a digestive problem that leaves him unable to digest his food fully first time around. In a multi-dog household you may need to check that your other dogs are not in need of digestive support. If they are unable to process their food, their faeces may seem more attractive.

Make sure your dog is eating enough, as a hungry dog is more likely to eat anything he can. Talk to a vet who specializes in nutrition and who can prescribe probiotics to improve gut function if necessary. Be prepared to experiment with your dog's diet, making any changes slowly so that his digestive tract has a chance to adapt. It is vital that your dog is getting the best quality food and that it can digest it easily; the foods we recommend are listed on page 126.

Meanwhile, teach your dog a 'leave' or 'off' cue so that you can divert his attention without having to shout at him, and quietly clean up the mess. Keep on top of clearing away any mess in the garden as well. Telling him off may encourage him to become more secretive or frantic about it. While it is generally more common in younger dogs, older dogs can develop the habit.

TTouches

- *Ear Work*
- *Belly Lifts*
- *Mouth Work*

Ginny is an old lady and recently developed coprophagia. A trip to the vet showed that she had slight pancreatitis, which was treated, and she now behaves in a more ladylike fashion!

Related ideas...   1   18

Claiming the furniture

It is important for your dog to understand social rules, and it is definitely not acceptable for him to growl or snap when asked to vacate a chair for ancient Auntie Mabel who is considering leaving everything to you in her will. But dogs learn by copying those around them, and if you don't want your dog to follow suit when you relax on your sofa you need to give him an alternative option.

Archie loves the sofa.

TTouches

- *Ear Slides*
- *Clouded Leopard TTouches over the whole body and around the hindquarters*
- *Tail Work*
- *Python Lifts down all four limbs*
- *Zigzags*

Given the choice between a draughty wooden floor and a comfy chair, many dogs will make the same choice as their human companions. They are not being 'dominant'. Your dog needs somewhere comfortable to lie as an alternative, but it is not necessary to have a huge immovable dog bed in each room; folded duvets work really well.

If your dog is refusing to move off the couch shouting the word 'off' and pointing to the floor will not work, particularly if he doesn't know what 'off' means. The chances are that you will unnerve him. If you try to wrestle him off he may roll on his back and urinate or snap at your hands.

Go back to basic training and teach him what 'Off' or 'Get down' means by using a clicker and rewarding him for doing as you ask. Use the ground work exercise on raised boards to practise it. You can also use clicker training to teach him to target his own bed consistently on a light-toned cue such as 'On your bed'. The TTouches listed will help to enhance his concentration and ability to learn.

Attach a light lead to your dog's collar and train him to come off the couch when requested. There is no need to loom over him or shout; if he does not get down, pick up the lead and call him to you calmly. The dog will soon learn that you can quietly and consistently enforce your request. Practice this frequently (don't wait until you have a houseful of guests) to ensure that your dog will vacate the couch and settle on his own comfy bed when asked.

If you loom over your dog you will make him nervous and he will be reluctant to move.

Look in the direction that you want him to go and click and treat him when he does as he is asked.

Related ideas...　　2　　58　　59　　93

Picky eating

Unless there is an underlying medical condition, most dogs get over faddy eating habits relatively easily. Picky eating can be a common problem in elderly dogs and can have a number of causes. Making sure your dog gets enough exercise and changing to a natural, wholesome diet usually does the trick.

Many elderly dogs suffer from stiffness associated with rheumatism and arthritis or have balance problems, such as vestibular disease, and they may find it difficult to lower their heads to eat. They can also lose sensation in their mouths and have difficulty picking up and chewing food without dropping it. Raising the food bowl is a simple way to make life easier. You should also check that your dog's teeth and gums are healthy, as a sore mouth will definitely put him off even his favourite meal.

Feeding the right amount

Some dogs find a full bowl overwhelming, particularly as they age and need to eat less. Try giving a smaller amount and clear away any food that is not consumed within 20 minutes. Your dog will probably eat his next meal with more gusto.

Don't leave food available at all times and monitor the number of treats you give during the day: your dog may well be getting all that he needs in rewards and small meals.

Avoid pouring gravy or stock over the food to tempt the dog to eat. Unless you have made it yourself, it is likely to be very high in salt and detrimental to your dog's health.

Ear Work can reduce stress and increase appetite.

You can also try doing slow circular Abalone TTouches on the belly.

TIP

You can try warming the food, particularly if it has been stored in a refrigerator, so that it smells more appealing to the dog. Cold food may not have much aroma.

USEFUL GROUND WORK EXERCISES

Raised poles to increase flexibility through the neck and back

Labyrinth

TTouches

- *Mouth Work*
- *Ear Slides*
- *Belly Lifts*
- *Abalone TTouches on stomach*
- *Lifts down hind limbs*
- *Raccoon TTouches down either side of the spine*

Related ideas...   1   11   39   40

Stealing food

As with all unwanted behaviours there are several reasons why dogs counter-surf or raid the kitchen cupboards, from nutritional deficiencies to a history of starvation or scavenging for food. Whatever the reason, this habit can be a bit of a nightmare and is also dangerous as the dog may ingest something that can make him ill. Certain foods can also be fatal for some dogs.

You must be realistic and fair: leaving a dog alone in the kitchen when food is present is a HUGE temptation. Teach him an 'off' or 'leave' cue using the clicker and treats, so that he learns that paws on counters (whether two or four!) are not appropriate. Avoid giving him tidbits when you are cooking as this will teach him that good things come from counters. Some dogs don't like the feel or sound of foil beneath their paws, so try putting some along the edges of your counters to inhibit jumping up, or try double-sided sticky tape.

With more mental and physical stimulation, your dog will settle more readily and will have less interest in making up his own entertainment. Giving him part of his food while doing tricks or tasks can make mealtimes more rewarding, and more tiring. Interactive dog games will encourage him to work for his food, and some dogs enjoy eating from a stuffed Kong. If he enjoys searching, let him watch you scatter some food in the garden – he will have a wonderful time finding it.

Archie is a fantastic thief and will steal on cue! He used to be appalling and could reach food in the most inaccessible places. Reducing his stress levels and giving him an appropriate diet helped to reduce this behaviour.

Related ideas... 1 40

Food bolting

40

A dog that bolts food may once have needed to eat quickly to guarantee he had his fill before his canine friends muscled in. He may have been starved, or he may have led a very dull existence, and the arrival of the supper bowl was the highlight of his day. He may be in need of worming, or be deficient in nutrients and therefore permanently hungry; he may even have a medical problem.

Check that his diet is appropriate for his breed and level of activity. Dogs that gobble their food in seconds are likely to be left feeling hungry if they only get one meal a day. Try splitting the daily food ration into two or three portions so that he does not have to wait so long between meals.

To slow the pace at which he eats, spread the food out on a plastic mat, teach him to look for scattered food and/or stuff part of his meal into a large Kong. You could also try putting a large stone into his dish so that he has to eat around it.

Dogs that bolt their food are often vocal and may carry tension through the jaw. Use the TTouches listed and a face-wrap to release tension in this area and to increase mind/body-awareness.

USEFUL GROUND WORK EXERCISES

Labyrinth – lay a few tasty morsels around it so that he learns to eat following a few calm, controlled strides.

TTouches

- *Any TTouches that will help to chill the dog out*
- *Mouth Work*
- *Belly Lifts*
- *Abalone TTouches on the belly*

Related ideas... 21 41

Living in a multi-dog household

Dogs generally enjoy living together, especially if they have had the opportunity to meet for the first time on neutral territory. Making sure that *all* your dogs are taught your house rules using reward-based methods will help each of them to build a bond with you as well as each other. This is particularly important with siblings who have been together since birth.

TTouches

- *Abalone along the midline and around the belly*

- *Python Lifts along the neck and back*

- *Clouded Leopard TTouches all over the body*

- *Chimp, Raccoon and Clouded Leopard around the muzzle and face*

- *Tail Work*

- *Ear Work*

We both live in multi-dog households and do not have any problems. We train our dogs to behave appropriately around us and with each other.

Dogs generally sort out minor squabbles, so there's no need to panic about the odd disagreement, but if your home begins to resemble a war zone you will need to become part of the peace process. Dogs are individuals and express concern in different ways, so look at the whole picture: for example, the dog with the loudest behaviour may be anxious about another dog's quiet pain.

A dog may become less tolerant if he is sore, so ensure that medical problems are treated or ruled out at an early stage. Elderly dogs can be overwhelmed by youngsters rushing around and can often get bumped or knocked over. Take extra care to avoid this at times of natural excitement like mealtimes or when the doorbell rings. An old dog will really appreciate the security of a quiet, comfy spot to rest while he watches the youngsters dashing around.

Hormones will also affect entire bitches and dogs and most shelters in the UK sensibly neuter their animals or request that new owners do the same at an appropriate age. Neutering dogs that have already developed issues with each other will not necessarily resolve the problem however and you will need to monitor interactions to prevent any conflicts from escalating. Watch for small signs and triggers. It isn't always the most vocal dog that instigates a fight. You may think that one particular dog is the cause of the problem when he in fact may have been triggered by a quieter dog staring at him in a threatening way.

They love playing together…

…but also appreciate some one-to-one time.

Resources can be a trigger for conflict and these include toys, your attention, a comfortable bed and food. Lack of space can also cause problems and dogs may also re-direct their concerns onto another dog if they are upset by noise or other stimuli. Observation is the key. Look for a pattern to see if the fight starts by dogs moving through a doorway together, if they have been playing a game, if one is tired and so on. Allow them to have plenty of space, provide at least one more bed than you have dogs and work with the dogs using TTouch and clicker training on their own basis to ensure that they have some special one to one attention.

TTouches

TTouch improves posture and self confidence and this can be a vital part of resolution. In the human world bullies pick on people they view as victims and the same can be true of dogs. Helping a timid dog to be more relaxed in both his mind and his body can reduce his chances of being picked on. Enlist the help of other family members or friends so that you can also work with the dogs together using TTouch and slow ground work exercises to teach them that good things can happen in each other's company.

We have had great success in using TTouch to resolve issues in multi-dog households but you will need to be realistic if the problem is serious. We have heard many horror stories of dogs killing other dogs that they have lived with, even after several years, and some dogs, like people, just don't get on. Orsa came to live with Sarah because she fell out with one particular dog, Grace, in her previous home. Orsa mixes well with all other canines and welcomes visiting dogs and foster puppies with open paws but when she saw Grace in the distance at a Maremma fun day she made it very clear that murder was still on her mind. They hadn't seen each other for two years and Orsa had never displayed this behaviour before or since. It was quite alarming for all those who witnessed this complete change in character but was confirmation to her original owner that she had done the right thing in rehoming her dog.

TIP
If one of your dogs eats more slowly than the others he may feel threatened and either defend his meal or leave it. Help the slow eater by supervising mealtimes until everybody has finished or by feeding him in a crate or separate room.

USEFUL GROUND WORK EXERCISES

Weave cones

Raised poles

Labyrinth

Spiral

Related ideas…

24   26   50

42

Cats

Teaching a dog to live happily alongside a feline friend largely depends on three things: the dog, the cat, and you. If you have a dog with a highly developed chase drive and a fearful cat, the chances of them snoozing together on the sofa are a little slim. But with diligent management, patience and a calm approach, miracles can happen.

You must be realistic. If your elderly or timid cat has previously enjoyed a peaceful existence he may really struggle with the new arrival. If you do not know much about your dog's past, it may be that he has already killed or seriously maimed a cat, so please bear this in mind.

Before they meet

Work with the animals separately at first, using the TTouches listed on both, and monitor their arousal levels. While you are keeping them apart, try putting some of your dog's bedding in the room with your cat and vice versa so that they become accustomed to each other's scent. Use clicker training to teach your dog a 'Leave' or 'Off' cue. You also need to know that you can get his attention, so teach him to target and follow your hand and to look at you (see page 28).

Introducing the animals

Set yourself up for success by making sure that your dog has had some exercise and is calm. If your cat is happy in a cat carrier pop him into it and put it on a table in a quiet room. If the carrier is an open cage, cover it so that your cat can hide if necessary.

Bring the dog to the doorway on a harness and lead and quietly stroke his ears and do your TTouch work. If he goes bananas, take him quietly away and calm him down. Repeat a few times until he is able to settle. Monitor your cat for signs of stress. If your dog is unable to get past this stage you will have to consider whether it is fair to keep him.

If your dog is calm around the cat, walk him nearer, still doing TTouches. Ask him to look at you, walk away on cue, sit and so on. Reward all quiet behaviour and give both cat and dog plenty of breaks.

Get a friend to do TTouches on the cat while you work with your dog, keeping him on the lead. Allow the cat to move if he wants to but make sure he has a place to hide or escape, and that your dog is safe from the cat's claws and teeth.

Progress to having your cat and dog together in the room but keep a line on your dog in case you need to remove him and do not be tempted to rush the friendship.

Bud was encouraged to chase cats from his garden in his previous home. Keeping him at a safe distance enables Sarah to work with him and mark any calming with her clicker while Marie does TTouches on the ever patient Angel.

Case History

HERBIE

If you have the time to continue building up their trust in each other, you have a good chance of helping a dog and cat to live side by side, as Sue shows in this letter:

Hi Sarah,

We were having difficulties with Herbie the terrier and our cat Dylan. Our previous dog had been very accepting and gentle with Dylan but Herbie was a 'different kettle of fish' and sadly our cat was feeling unable to even enter the house (this we felt guilty about).

Having attended your fantastic workshop I have set about applying some of the TTouches, especially in the presence of Dylan. Although Herbie still gets a little 'excited' when he hears the cat flap, things have improved dramatically. Dylan

has also gained confidence, because he now realizes that Herbie will not actually hurt him.

I have attached a photo of the harmony that now exists!!

Regards, Sue

Bud is settling well and is focus is now on Sarah and the treats as opposed to Angel. By choice Bud also started to back away which was also rewarded as a more appropriate behaviour to lunging forward.

TTouches

- *Ear Slides*
- *Mouth Work*
- *Slow Zigzags*
- *Raccoon TTouches around the shoulders*
- *Tail Work*
- *Stroking with the wand*

USEFUL GROUND WORK EXERCISES

Labyrinth

Related ideas... 33   79   81   85

Stealing

As with children, it is all too easy to ignore the right things that our dogs do and focus on the things that they do wrong. If your dog is not acknowledged for playing with and chewing his toys and bones but gets a huge amount of attention if he picks up a remote control or a pair of glasses, guess which he is going to choose. It's even more fun if you join in the game by chasing him.

TTouches

- *Mouth Work*
- *Connected circles all over the body to help build the bond*

Stealing is a common attention-seeking behaviour that often starts young. The first and most important step is to teach your dog to play a shared game, giving up his toy on the 'Off' or 'Leave' cue. Acknowledge and praise your clever dog when he chews his own toys or bones. If he picks up something he shouldn't, call him to you, make a fuss of him, ask him to release your treasure and replace it with one of his own. This can quickly resolve the problem behaviour.

Some dogs, however, especially rescue dogs, steal something to get attention and then panic if a human looks annoyed, and will often hide the article or chew it. If this is the case you may need to become more creative. Find a few objects that are safe to chew and you do not mind sacrificing. It doesn't matter what they are, but you need to convince your dog that they are precious to you.

Put anything really special right out of reach and substitute them with the decoy articles. When your dog picks one up, react as if he is stealing something valuable to you. After a few days, stop reacting. Try not to acknowledge his behaviour in any way, but pay him lots of attention and give him lots of praise when he picks up one of his own toys.

Dogs learn to repeat anything that gains your attention, and they love a game of chase.

Case History
ARCHIE

Sarah's dog Archie was a stray from Battersea Dogs and Cats Home. He had multiple unwanted behaviours, and one was that he would snatch any grooming equipment he found on the barn floor when Sarah and the livery owners were with their horses. The sight of him trotting past the barn doors with his trophies in his mouth, furry ears a-flap, desperate for someone to chase him, was hilarious but his behaviour was annoying for everyone who was trying to groom their horses. Sarah set out some old unwanted brushes and just ignored him. It worked a treat.

Teach your dog that it can be more fun playing with something he is allowed to have.

Related ideas...   21   39

The delivery man

Service providers who visit the home on a regular basis can become the target of the family dog and are frequently bitten. Many owners think this is because their dog has been tormented, but this is very rarely the case.

We (hopefully) teach our dogs to accept visitors as safe once they enter our home, so dogs are most likely to guard at entrance doors and garden gates. Your dog may bark as someone comes up the path, and bark even more furiously if they put something through the door. As far as he is concerned, his barking results in the visitor quickly disappearing. He may have daily opportunities to practice this behaviour, so if he gains access to a delivery man who is brazenly standing his ground it is hardly surprising if he snaps or bites in an effort to chase the intruder away.

In theory, it might help to get somebody wearing an appropriate uniform to greet your dog confidently and take time to offer treats and make friends. But you would need a number of people to do this over a period of time to generalize the behaviour. Instead, responsible dog owners ensure that their dogs do not have access to the front door when the mail is due, and most dogs are happy to be relieved of the responsibility.

TTouch

TTouch work can help to keep a dog more settled, and teaching him games and new skills will give him other outlets for his instincts. You can also try using treats to change his association with the sound of the letterbox or doorbell, but you need to consider the implications of this: if there are constant callers in your absence your dog may become more frustrated.

It is really important that you teach a good recall so that you can remove him from the gate as it is not always safe or appropriate to touch a dog if he in is a high state of alert or really aroused. Dragging a dog by his collar may trigger him to become more agitated and he may even bite you. Shouting at him could tell him that you too are concerned about the presence of the stranger and his behaviour could escalate. Use your TTouches and/or ground work to settle the dog after the event as stress levels may continue to rise long after the delivery man has gone.

Leo loves TTouch and it is an excellent way of reducing his arousal levels as he matures into an adult dog.

Leo is a guardian breed. A good recall, training and plenty of exercise is essential to keep him focused and content.

TTouches

- Ear Slides
- Clouded Leopard TTouches along the back and around the hindquarters
- Tail Work
- Mouth Work

USEFUL GROUND WORK EXERCISES

Working between barriers

Raised or uneven poles

Labyrinth

Related ideas... 45 60 67 70 71

Inappropriate greetings

Dogs, like people, use their mouths to express themselves. When overexcited or anxious, gundog breeds in particular have a desperate need to carry something in their mouths, and some dogs learn to take hold of a person's arm or hand when they meet them. But this is a dangerous habit as not everyone will interpret it as friendly, and even if your dog is soft-mouthed it can hurt.

Monty really hurts when he grabs an arm in a greeting.

It is extremely important to teach your dog to release anything that he is holding with a *calm* one-word cue such as 'Leave' or 'Off'. Teaching him to greet you by touching your hand with his nose can also be helpful (see page 51).

The desire to carry something is instinctive for many dogs, and they generally prefer it to be soft. Offer an appropriate toy and praise him when he is carrying it. Use TTouches to help him settle more quickly when you or your visitors walk through the door. If you are struggling to teach your dog an alternative behaviour, try using a face-wrap to make him more aware of his habit and improve his focus. It might also be worth checking your house insurance!

Giving him his own duck to hold allows him an outlet for this natural behaviour.

Case History
TOBY

Some years ago Marie came home laden with bags and failed to notice that her adolescent Golden Retriever Toby was unable to find anything to carry and present to her in greeting. A terrible grating noise ensued and Marie turned to see Toby proudly dragging the huge floor rug towards her, with the sideboard that was standing on it in tow, ornaments flying. After that, she made sure Toby always had something safe to present to returning family and visitors.

TTouches

- *Ear Slides*
- *Chimp TTouch around muzzle*
- *Raccoon TTouches along jaw line and around base of ears and skull*
- *Tail Work*

TTouches around the chest and muzzle are very calming for Monty.

Related ideas...   46   47   48   60   63   73

Mouthing

Your dog will have learned about play biting in the litter from his mother, brothers and sisters. Puppies spend lots of time mouthing and play fighting and learn how to control their bite through their interaction with their siblings. It is important to continue the puppy's education when he leaves the litter.

A puppy needs to learn quickly that play biting, although natural, is not an appropriate way to interact with humans. If he becomes overexcited and begins to bite you, however softly, exclaim 'Ouch!' and briefly withdraw from him. A young dog will usually look surprised and immediately try to lick you. If this happens, ignore him for 30 seconds, then call him to you. If he play bites again, repeat the procedure until he makes the connection between his behaviour and the withdrawal of your attention.

Some dogs however, find it rather stimulating to have a large human squeaky toy, and may escalate their behaviour if you make a noise. If this is the case leave the room and shut the door behind you, without looking at or speaking to the dog. Stay out of the room for a couple of minutes and when you go back remain neutral if he approaches you. Repeat these steps if necessary until he really understands the link between his behaviour and the loss of your attention. When he is calm, call him to you and resume your game. If you are consistent in your responses the behaviour will soon extinguish.

TTouch and ground work

Use the TTouches to help to calm him, and progress to working around his muzzle to help him learn some self-control. You can also use any slow ground work exercises to give him another way of learning to interact with you calmly.

Cookie Dough Dynamo was dropped off at Battersea Dogs and Cats Home when very young. She was probably taken too early from her mother and had not learned how to control her mouth when interacting with people.

TTouches

- *Chimp TTouches around the muzzle*
- *Ear Slides*
- *Raccoon TTouches either side of the head*

Cookie Dough quickly learnt to play with toys and to enjoy hand contact.

She also learnt to target a hand with her nose, giving her a more appropriate way of communicating with people.

Related ideas...   47   48   49

47 Avoid rough games

It is not fair to encourage your dog to play games that may get him into serious trouble if he tries to play them with somebody else. You may end up in court, but he could pay with his life. If you teach a good one-word release cue you can have just as much fun playing tugging games with an appropriate toy.

Layla is typical of many dogs that have learnt to play roughly with people; she drew blood on several occasions.

Sometimes when a dog is becoming aroused, his gums and the white of the eye will redden and/or his eye may appear glazed and hard. If you notice these changes, stop whatever might have triggered the arousal and let him calm down.

If you have adopted a dog that has already been encouraged to play rough games, wait until he is calm then use TTouch body work and ground work combined with clicker training to help him learn more self-control.

Teaching Layla the joys of playing with toys was a vital part of her rehabilitation.

USEFUL GROUND WORK EXERCISES

Different surfaces

Raised poles

Labyrinth

Fan

Weave cones

TTouches

- *Chimp TTouch around the muzzle*
- *Raccoon TTouches around the jaw line*
- *Ear Slides*
- *Lying Leopard TTouches and Lifts along the ribs, belly and back*
- *Clouded Leopard TTouches either side of breastbone*
- *Lying Leopard TTouches on top of skull*

TTouch was another really useful tool for calming Layla when she became overexcited.

Related ideas...   46   48   58

Ragging on clothing

Many young dogs get themselves into trouble for ragging on trousers and biting toes and ankles. Moving feet and flapping material can be very exciting for playful puppies. Mouthing and biting clothing or hair should receive the same response as biting skin.

Chloe is a typical young pup whose natural instincts are to hold everything in her mouth. Marie is putting a harness on Chloe and Chloe is becoming agitated.

If your dog has already developed this habit, avoid pushing him away with your feet as this will make the game more exciting. If you are unable to withdraw your attention and move into another room, teach him to wear a harness and keep a light house-line attached to enable you to contain him without escalating his behaviour by touching him.

It doesn't necessarily follow that a dog that rags on clothing will become a wild savage, but you do need to teach him an alternative and more rewarding way of interacting with you to prevent the problem from getting out of control. Work on his training when he is calm so that he can focus and learn. It is

easy to forget to reward your dog when he is quiet, but click and treat him at every opportunity when he has four feet on the ground and he is not grabbing any part of your clothing. Drop the treats onto the floor so that he takes his focus away from your body. Remember to reward all his appropriate behaviours so that he does not need to get your attention through rough play, and repeat this many times during the day. It is worth the effort.

Teaching him to target a stick, such as the super training clicker and treat dispenser developed by Mary Ray (see Suppliers, page 126), can be useful for shaping all sorts of behaviours. You can also teach him to target a mat and to interact with you in a more rewarding way such as with a gentle hand touch greeting, using the techniques shown in *100 Ways to Train the Perfect Dog*.

This should create a window of opportunity for you to begin some TTouch and containing exercises to help him to stand still. A head wrap helps to calm some dogs, and if he is resistant because there is tension in this area, Chimp TTouches around the base of the ears and around the hinge point for the jaw may be useful. As he calms you can change to more specific TTouches around his head and at the base of his skull.

TTouches

- *Llama and Chimp TTouch around the muzzle*
- *Slow Zigzags over the body*
- *Light Springbok TTouches all over the body and around the top of the head*

Marie quietens Chloe using a gentle containment and TTouch work which will help to reduce her over excitable behaviours when aroused.

Marie is able to put the harness on a calm Chloe. Her 'play' behaviour of ragging on trousers and sleeves is also quickly diminishing.

USEFUL GROUND WORK EXERCISES

Weave cones

Raised boards

Labyrinth

Related ideas...   **45**   **46**   **47**

49 Teach your dog to play with you

Some dogs have never learnt to play because they lacked early social interaction with humans. Others may have been scared by a rough game, or frightened by their owner's reaction when they picked something up as a puppy. TTouch is a wonderful way to start the bonding process and develop trust, and ground work exercises will help your dog gain confidence.

Sharing a game is twice the fun – Oz races back to Marie with his toy.

TIP
If your dog shows no interest in balls or raggies, you can teach him other games such as searching for food or playing with the Nina Ottosson interactive dog toys. Most dogs will work for interesting tidbits, so there is still fun to be had.

Clicker training is a good way to teach your dog to play with toys. Patience is the key. You will need some small tasty treats and a comfortable place to sit; you will also need an interesting toy. We like homemade fleecy plaits because it is long enough for both the dog and the owner to hold whilst allowing you to keep a little distance from each other to prevent your hand being grabbed by mistake. You can also stuff a few treats into the plaits to trigger the dog's curiosity as you want to encourage him to interact with the toy and not view it with suspicion or disdain.

Lay the toy on the floor between you and the dog. Mark any movement he makes towards the toy with your clicker and throw him a treat. You want to reward any interest he shows in it even if it is a quick glance at or head turn towards it. Even if his focus is on you and not the toy, mark any movement he makes that takes him nearer the toy – whether he is aware of its presence or not – and then wait to see if he pays it any attention. He doesn't have to touch it at this stage,

Click and treat your dog when he makes any move towards the toy.

but you do want to start shaping his behaviour. Put the toy away before he becomes bored or switches off; you want it to remain interesting so that you can develop the exercise. Do not be afraid to repeat these simple steps, and remember to keep the sessions short.

Once he understands that the toy and the rewards are linked you can pick up the toy and reward any move he makes towards it whilst it is in your hand. Click and treat each step until he is happy to hold it in his mouth while you hold the other end in your hand. Build his confidence until he is happy to hold his end of the toy in his mouth while you do some TTouch work with your spare hand and chat to him. Stay calm and don't ruffle his ears or pat him excitedly as you may scare him. Gradually build on this good foundation so that he can play with you and his toy. Teach him an 'off' or 'leave' cue, and develop the game further by teaching him to retrieve. All these exercises are shown in *100 ways to Train the Perfect Dog*.

Cookie is beginning to realize that the toy is key to her food rewards.

She is a fast learner and is already bringing back another toy to share with Marie.

TTouches

- Chimp TTouches around the muzzle
- Mouth Work
- Tail Work
- Raccoon TTouches around the jaw and back of the neck
- Clouded Leopard TTouches around the hindquarters

USEFUL GROUND WORK EXERCISES

Different surfaces

Teeter totter

Raised board

Related ideas... 50 65 81

Reluctance to play with other dogs

You dog may not have been well socialized with other dogs and could be anxious about playing doggy games. Avoid the temptation to gabble in a high pitched 'encouraging' voice; he won't be fooled and may think that you are anxious about the other dog too which will make him even more suspicious of playing.

Never force your dog into a situation because you think it will help him to learn how to play; it could tip him over the edge and result in him lunging or barking defensively at the other dog. By all means introduce him to quiet, well-balanced dogs by letting him approach them, but do not be surprised if he advances and retreats quite a few times before he actually gets close.

Make sure he has the choice to escape and back away if necessary. It is a perfectly natural and sensible thing for him to do while he evaluates whether the other dog is safe. Your dog may quickly gain confidence and respond to

Dogs that are fearful hold tension in the hindquarters, and TTouch work is brilliant for helping them to feel more confident in the presence of other dogs.

another dog's invitation to play, or it may take a few meetings before he feels brave enough to romp around. There are no hard and fast rules; we do not like every other person that we meet and the same applies to dogs, so give him space and time to decide whether or not he wants to make a friend.

USEFUL GROUND WORK EXERCISES

Labyrinth
– you can walk two dogs together in labyrinths laid parallel, but not too close

Weave cones

TTouches

- *Ear Slides*
- *Clouded Leopard TTouches around hindquarters*
- *Tail Work*
- *Raccoon TTouches around neck*
- *Clouded Leopard TTouches around the chest*

Her new owner learns some TTouches so that she can continue to help her dog. Ryan from the Blue Cross is ably assisted by his very calm dog Ringo.

Related ideas... 33 41 79

Negotiating stairs

Many accidents have occurred when a young dog has tried to negotiate stairs, and this may have a lasting physical impact on him if he damages his spine or joints.

It is also unpleasant (and dangerous) for owners if they are barged out of the way by a hairy bullet that is charging down the staircase behind them or enthusiastically leading the way down a flight of external steps. Bear in mind that polished wooden steps, wet slippery steps or open steps where the dog can see the ground below are going to be more challenging to your four legged friend.

The speed with which a dog negotiates stairs is based on his coordination. Ground work is a simple way to help him learn to organize his body more effectively without gravity taking over, and to develop better paw/eye coordination. Use the clicker to mark slow, considered movement, and teach a 'Steady' cue.

A harness and/or balance-lead will help your dog learn how to move his centre of gravity backwards through his body when doing the ground work, and will also help when teaching him to walk calmly down a flight of steps. Use a body-wrap to give him better balance.

Find a short flight of steps to keep the exercise simple.

Cookie has been taught to walk downstairs slowly using the clicker.

Ground work formed a major part of Cookie's early education, and she has excellent balance and good self-control as a result.

TTouches

- *Zigzags to help him connect through the body*

- *Tail Work to improve movement through the hips*

- *Python Lifts down the legs*

- *Leg circles to loosen stiff hindquarters*

USEFUL GROUND WORK EXERCISES

Pick up sticks

Fan

Uneven poles

Labyrinth

Teeter totter

Raised boards

Different surfaces

Related ideas... 56

Dislike of contact

The fabulous Fred came to Tilley Farm to be the model for this section. His owner Mina, has worked wonders with this little terrier and we all fell in love with him. Mina and Sarah had been emailing each other prior to the visit and Mina took Fred for a health check at her vet's before the session.

Fred's story is a classic one. Multiple issues, multiple homes. The reason that he came to Tilley Farm was because Mina cannot always touch her gorgeous dog and he has bitten on several occasions. As is so common in issues with being stroked and handled, Fred had a physical problem and was put on pain relief for hip dysplasia. If your dog has any worries about being handled, we recommend that you take him to your vet for a thorough examination as pain is often the cause of this behaviour. Other reasons may also include fear due to a lack of being handled appropriately as a puppy, early parts of his training and socialisation being overlooked or the memory of a bad experience in the past. Diet may also be a factor as hot, itchy skin can be further aggravated by being patted or stroked and older dogs may be suffering from joint pain which will reduce their tolerance. Whatever the origin of the problem, there is always a valid reason why dogs dislike being touched and it is tragic that some people overlook all these probable reasons and label the dog as 'dominant.'

If your dog is fearful about being touched, forcing contact upon him will do little to allay his concerns. A quiet approach, breaking the sessions down into small steps, is the way forward. This will enable you to develop a relationship with your dog based on trust and understanding, and TTouch body work and ground work exercises are just perfect for helping dogs learn that contact from a human can be pleasant and highly rewarding.

Initiating contact

Different breeds have different ways of expressing themselves and hounds, for example, will tend to shut down, leading you to believe they are enjoying the attention. Other dogs, such as collies, often freeze (as do other breeds), while the Bull family may go into fool around mode and become excitable. If you watch for early signs of concern you can work slowly and carefully with your dog and avoid inadvertently pushing him to the point where he has to use more obvious body language such as biting or nipping.

Make sure that your dog is not in his bed or cornered when you initiate contact. This will naturally make him feel more threatened. Avoid stroking him when you are standing or sitting directly in front of him, and keep to the side of your dog, provided it is safe to do so. This is far less alarming to a worried dog than a hand that is reaching out directly over the top of his head.

Vigorous patting or ruffling of the coat may make him more concerned, so try stroking him gently with the back of your hand. Pay close attention to his body language. If he starts licking his lips, holding his breath or panting for example it is likely that he is unsure about the experience.

If you are unable to touch him with your hand, try using

TTouches

- *Stroking the ear against the dog's own body*
- *Llama TTouch*
- *Chimp TTouch*
- *Troika TTouch*
- *Half circle*

USEFUL GROUND WORK EXERCISES

Labyrinth

Different surfaces

Raised platform

Treats and free ground work, with no contact, can be a useful starting point for dogs that dislike being touched.

a wand. This is a white dressage schooling stick that TTouch practitioners use to initiate contact with a nervous animal. Starting with a wand enables you to keep your distance from the dog and also changes his expectation of what might happen. Watch his responses at all times and if there is any doubt do not use the wand. Some dogs have been beaten with sticks and holding something in your hand may be a trigger for defensive reactions.

You can also try using a fake hand. These can be made from joke rubber hands fixed on to a wooden stick, inside a stuffed shirt sleeve. The hand should be used as an extension of your own arm, and must obviously not be used to prod or goad the dog.

Some dogs do better when ground work exercises are incorporated into the handling process, and we have both helped dogs overcome their concerns by beginning with ground work and not touching the dog at all initially. The slow movement helps to reduce stress, improves circulation through the body and has therefore been a vital step for many dogs that were defensive when touched.

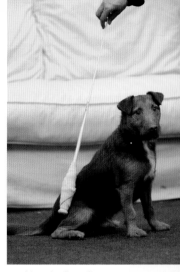

After introducing Fred gently to the wand by stroking the floor first, then touching his paw or shoulder, Sarah covered its end with a body-wrap and rolled it gently over Fred's back and hindquarters. She also began to fall in love with Fred.

Sarah asked Mina to stroke Fred with a second wand to give him lots of different experiences.

TIP

If your dog allows you to touch him but does not enjoy the experience or has sensitive areas, try covering your hand with a sheepskin mitt or a glove. Reducing the amount of heat your pet can feel in your hand is beneficial for many dogs.

Sarah also showed Mina how to do the TTouches so that she could continue to work with Fred at home.

Fred was worried by direct hand contact around his hindquarters, so Sarah started working on his shoulders.

Related ideas... 23 54 59

Indoor kennels

Dogs can learn to settle in an indoor kennel provided the whole introduction exercise was set up in an appropriate way. If you have inherited a dog that is worried by this containment but really need to use an indoor kennel, you will have to go back to basics and teach him that a crate is a good and safe place to be.

Bear in mind that the kennel may have been used as a punishment in a previous home, may have been too small (this is quite common) or he may have been left in the crate for prolonged periods. Other dogs may naturally be concerned about lying under anything that has a roof; if they are wary of people or suspicious of new situations they may feel insecure about having their vision restricted.

Open bed training

Get your dog used to sleeping in an open bed by teaching him the 'settle' cue as shown in *100 Ways to Train the Perfect Dog*. He will probably be happier if the bed is in a corner of a quiet room. Invest in some plywood and make a wooden base with a low back for stability and fix a taller wooden board made from ply on one side. Put your dog's bed on the wooden board so that he learns to sleep next to a solid side. Make sure it is securely fixed as he could be scared and/or hurt if it topples over. Once he is happy with this arrangement add a board to the other side so that he learns to sleep in between two boards. You should now have a something that resembles a large wooden dog bed with a low back and higher sides. If he becomes suspicious of his bed at any point go back a step or make the sides lower. You can always add an extra piece of wood later to increase the height. Continue developing his confidence by placing a light sheet or length of material over the end of the boards which can gradually be brought forward over time, so that he becomes accustomed to sleeping under a cover. Make sure that the material is always securely fixed so that it does not droop down and touch him, as this may alarm him. Make sure that he has chew toys or a stuffed Kong in his bed so that he enjoys resting in it.

Use a crate that gives him plenty of room to move around,

Once your dog is confident to lie in his bed at each stage you can move on through the exercise. If he panics at any point don't be afraid to go back a few steps.

lie down flat out and stand without causing him any concern. Place his bed inside the crate and cover it with his sheet. so that it looks the same as his covered resting place.

Leave the door open so that he can come and go at will, and make sure that he has access to clean water and chew toys at all times.
Pull the cover slightly over the front of the crate so that he can still come and go without feeling trapped, but is becoming accustomed to having to walk through a slightly narrower space to enter his bed.

Push the door slightly closed when he is truly confident about spending time in the crate, but do not shut him in until he feels really content to be in an enclosed space. Avoid rushing any part of the exercise and if in doubt go back to the step where he was most comfortable.

Try a half-wrap or doggy T-shirt so that he has better body and spatial awareness.

TIP

Make sure no one bothers your dog when he is resting. Children in particular need to learn that a dog should be left in peace when in bed.

USEFUL GROUND WORK EXERCISES

Different surfaces

Labyrinth

Walking between two boards

Walking under sheeting

TTouches

- Ear Slides
- Clouded Leopard TTouches over the whole body
- Mouth work

Related ideas...   27   55

Containment

Dogs that have concerns about being held in place, picked up, or restrained in any way – including on the lead – will also often have issues with being towel dried, wearing a harness, being hugged, being touched by people unknown to him, being in an indoor kennel, being groomed, travelling in a car and being examined by a judge or a veterinarian.

If you are struggling with a dog that has these problems and you have been told he is asserting his authority over you, ask yourself if you know any people that dislike being hugged or feel threatened when people come into their personal space. If you do, would you label them as dominant or would you understand that they might have a problem?

Start slowly

Begin with the steps for stroking your dog. If you cannot touch him at all it makes sense that he would panic if you try to restrain him. Use the ground work exercises to help him move through poles and boards; teaching a dog to walk through narrow spaces can be the easiest way to start helping him to overcome his concerns.

Once you can safely touch your dog, try doing the Touches with a body-wrap held in your hand. Fold the body-wrap and drape it over his shoulders. When he is comfortable with this step, tie it loosely around his neck – you will need to fold the wrap in half unless you own a dog the size of a horse.

Do some belly lifts with the wrap; if he is nervous about this step, tie one end of the wrap onto the far end of the wand and let him walk over the body-wrap on the ground. You can stroke him under his belly with the wand and also stroke him all over with the wrap. The aim is to progress to picking up the trailing end of the wrap and hold it in the same hand as the wand, while the wrap is under the dog's rib cage, so that you have a body-wrap hammock. Try doing lifts with the wrap while it is attached to the wand. If he panics you can quietly lower the wand and ask him to step out of the hammock.

If he is happy, take the wrap off the wand and tie it in a figure of eight around the chest, over the shoulders and under the ribcage. Keep the wrap loose. Continue using the ground work exercises so that you incorporate movement into this exercise. This will be easier for some dogs as they may panic if your total focus is on them accepting the wrap.

You can also try a loose fitting dog-coat if he is comfortable wearing a coat, and pop the wrap on over the coat.

Gradually build on the exercises over time, teaching him the containment exercises as shown in *100 Ways to Train the Perfect Dog*. Avoid rushing any of the steps and pay attention to his body language and any areas that are sensitive to contact at all times.

Once he is happy to wear a wrap, teach him to wear a TTouch harness or make one out of a rope. Avoid harnesses that involve something going over his head, ones that require you to lift his front legs or any equipment that tightens if the dog is pulling as this will frighten him.

TTouches

- *Troika TTouch*
- *Ear Slides*
- *Zigzags*
- *Clouded Leopard TTouches all over the body*
- *Leg Circles if safe to do so*
- *Python Lifts on shoulders, ribs and hindquarters*
- *Belly Lifts with wraps*
- *Abalone TTouches on the midline*
- *Back Lifts*

This lovely Rottweiler bitch is a very friendly dog but has coat changes and hair loss around her back ribs and hindquarters, which is likely to be the reason that she is very concerned about being held. Marie starts by doing some clicker training and TTouches to establish trust.

Marie then lays the body-wrap over the dog's body. Tying the end of it to a wand enables Marie to pass the wrap under the dog's belly to form a hammock with which she can do Belly Lifts.

Related ideas... 52 53 87

Accustom your dog to the television

Many dogs become reactive towards the television. This may start because they are sensitive to sound or flickering light from the strange box in the corner, or even because they associate it with family members becoming animated. The starting point in solving this issue is to help a dog be calm in the room when the television is off.

Some dogs become so excited and aroused that they grab at anything or anybody who happens to touch them or be close by when they become over stimulated by the flickering and sounds on the television. It is easier to contain your dog and help him to be calm if he is wearing a harness over a body-wrap or t-shirt, with two points of lead contact.

TTouch body work will help him to settle and to begin to feel relaxed in that environment. Click and treat calm behaviour in the room to start building up a reward history.

Bring the dog into the room when the television is switched on but with the sound off. Work with your dog at an appropriate distance from the television so that he is able to stay calm and non-reactive. Begin with boring films, using containment, TTouch and clicker training to help him to remain calm. Slowly increase the volume and keep working with your dog. It is important not to rush these steps by turning the sound up too quickly.

Gradually work towards the point where the dog can stay calm with more stimulating sights/sounds on the screen.

Oscar is a serial television attacker, becoming very aroused by both the sight and sound.

TIP

Teach your dog to settle with a stuffed Kong in a special spot in the room, where he is undisturbed by doors opening and people moving past him. Use the exercise in 100 Ways to Train the Perfect Dog to teach him to settle in that spot.

TTouches

- *Llama and Lying Leopard over the body*

- *Chimp TTouch to side of face and around the base of the ears*

- *Ear Slides*

- *Tail TTouches to quieten the tail*

- *Mouth Work to aid self-control and reduce barking*

Marie introduces the body-wrap and works with Oscar using TTouches with the television switched off to help him learn to settle in the room. She then puts the television on, and works behind a barrier so that the screen doesn't stimulate the dog, using the clicker and treats to reward all calm behaviours. It is a good idea to use a house-line and harness so that you can contain the dog.

Related ideas...   25   62

Barging through doorways

Dogs do not rush through doorways or gaps because they want to assert authority over people. They do not know that humans consider it to be bad manners if they launch through a doorway felling their owners with a swift blow to the back of the knees as they pass.

Being barged out of the way by an enthusiastic hound is unpleasant and dangerous.

Naomi drops treats on the floor to encourage Orsa to move away from the door.

Rushing can also indicate concern. As annoying as it may be, it is unfair to punish a dog if he has not been taught a more appropriate behaviour. He simply needs to learn some self-control and understand that walking calmly behind a person through small gaps is a more rewarding experience. It's easier for most dogs to start learning controlled behaviour using an internal door, as external doors often hold the promise of a walk or trip in the car.

With the dog on a light lead, walk to the door with him at your side and slightly behind you. A quick way to teach this is to drop a treat at your side but slightly behind you, then click as he moves towards it. If he tries to push forward, move back; as he begins to follow you, click and drop a treat to the side and slightly behind you. As he moves to take it, click and drop another treat in the same place.

Put your hand on the door handle. If he moves forward, take your hand away and remain still until he moves behind you again, then click and treat. Repeat until he is able to maintain this position calmly when you touch and then move the door handle.

Open the door a crack; if he rushes forward close the door and wait. When he moves behind you, click and drop a treat. Continue to shape this behaviour until you are able to open the door without your dog moving forward. Take one step forward. If he maintains his position, click and treat. If he makes a dash for the open door, stand still; he can't go far because he is on the lead. Stroke the lead and wait for him to come back and move behind you. Click and treat.

Continue to shape this behaviour until you are able to walk through the door with him to the side and slightly behind you. Generalize the behaviour by practising with other internal doors, then external doors. Complete the exercise by teaching him to follow you through other doors and gateways.

> **TIP**
> The TTouches and ground work exercises, useful for dogs that lack the confidence to walk through doorways (see next page), are also appropriate here.

Orsa sits patiently while Naomi opens the door.

Related ideas... **57**

Walking through doorways

Your dog may hang back from doorways because he has been caught by a door opening or closing in his face, had a paw or tail pinched, or it may simply be a case of poor spatial awareness. When dogs panic they lose awareness of their body, so use a body-wrap or T-shirt to improve awareness. TTouch body work can help a dog to be calm and focus again.

Attach a lead to contain your dog, but avoid pushing or pulling him. Use TTouch to help him to relax at a comfortable distance from the door, keeping the lead loose. Drop his favourite toy or a few of his favourite treats on the floor. Gradually move towards the door and continue to throw the toy or treats just in front of you. Remain neutral and be patient; if you try to hassle your dog to move forward he may get worried and freeze.

When he plucks up the courage to move through the doorway he will probably bolt through as quickly as possible. Allow him to do this a few times to build his confidence, but make sure the sudden movement does not catch you off guard. If you are bracing you may pull the lead back and hurt him, reinforcing his fears.

TIP
Use a body wrap to help give your dog better body and spatial awareness.

Case History

TAZ

Taz was suffering from some physical issues that affected his confidence to walk on slippery surfaces and through gaps. The caring Blue Cross staff covered his kennel floor with quilts and sheets, and laid a path of quilts through the kennel runs and out to the exercise area so that he could get out on to the grass.

He responded well to TTouch in the quiet, contained environment of his kennel and was also quite happy to wear a half body-wrap. When he ventured out of his kennel, a 2m (6ft) lead connected to his collar was looped in front of his chest to provide a balance-lead. This helped to give him some confidence as he learned to walk through the doorways of the outdoor runs and on to the grassed area.

Soon Taz was able to move forward and back through the door without the aid of a balance-lead. On returning to the block he walked over a bare tiled floor and went straight into his kennel.

Marie starts working with Taz in his kennel as he was unable to relax outside, and he begins to calm down.

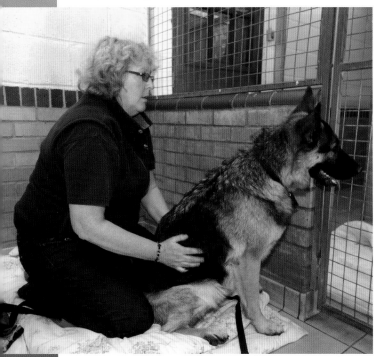

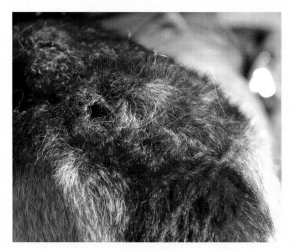

Coat changes can be indicative of injury or disease; Taz was indeed suffering from severe arthritis.

Taz is really worried about walking through the narrow doorway.

Taz starts to move more confidently through the doorway.

He is able to move freely through the door on his own.

USEFUL GROUND WORK EXERCISES

Balance-lead

Different surfaces

Walk-over poles

Labyrinth

Walking between barriers

TTouches

- Chimp TTouch around face, base of ears and muzzle
- Ear TTouch
- Mouth Work
- Clouded Leopard in connected circles along body and down legs
- Tail Work

Related ideas...   35   56   77

Sleeping through the night

Pain, separation anxiety and sensitivity to noise can be linked to this problem. A dog that is cold will also wake more, so trying to identify the possible causes of your dogs concern are going to go a long way to helping him to settle at night.

Case History

TESS

Maria was contacted by Anna to help her rescue dog Tess, a three-year-old Staffordshire Bull Terrier who had stopped wanting to go for walks (which she had previously loved) after being spooked by noise from a firing range. She was also worried about the vet, struggled in the car and was restless at night, running up and down stairs and barking at everything that passed the front door. She was totally fixated on Anna's husband Keith and became agitated when he left the house.

Initially Tess was very tense and allowed Maria to touch her only while she had eye contact with Keith, but as Maria used TTouches with slow strokes and light pressure, Tess's eyes softened and her breathing slowed. She still needed to keep checking in with Keith, but kept returning to Maria for TTouch.

Maria showed Anna and Keith how to do some TTouches, and when she left Tess was asleep on the sofa. Anna reported that Tess slept all night following that session – the first time she had done so in the nine months she had been living with them.

On a subsequent visit Maria initiated clicker training and Tess was very quick to pick up the principles. Maria fitted her with a T-shirt, harness and double-ended lead, and Tess walked straight out of the door and down the road. After further sessions she has calmed down, is able to travel in the car and enjoys her walks to the park.

Make sure that your dog is actually happy to rest in his bed during the day. He may avoid his bed, opting for an alternative place away from noise or draughts; changing the position of his sleeping quarters may be all that it takes to remedy this problem.

Outside noises are often louder and more intermittent at night. He may be listening to owls, or foxes calling or shouting in the street. Try leaving a radio playing classical music on low throughout the night to diffuse other sounds, and remember that dogs that are already in a state of stress will be more aroused by stimuli. You can also try a T-shirt or dog coat to help him sleep, but make sure he will not overheat or get himself caught up.

Use TTouch work to keep him calm and settled during the day and ensure that he is mentally and physically stimulated through exercise and appropriate games. Any ground work that you can set up in your garden will be of value, as slow movement helps dogs to become more relaxed in all areas of their lives. Shelter dogs that are stressed sleep well after a TTouch session, even though there is little that can be done to change their environment, so do not underestimate the power of this work. The body work will also help you to identify any stiff or sensitive areas, and will provide you with many ways of helping your dog to release tension. Dogs that are in a constant state of alert are usually exhausted and an over tired dog can be more restless than a dog that has slept on and off throughout the day. Remember to allow him some quiet time if he is leading a very active life.

USEFUL GROUND WORK EXERCISES

Labyrinth

Teeter totter

Raised boards

Different surfaces

Fan

A dog that has insufficient exercise will find it hard to settle at night, and many benefit from an evening stroll.

TTouches

- *Chimp TTouch around the head*

- *Ear Slides*

- *Tail Work*

- *Slow, connected Clouded and Lying Leopard TTouches all over the body*

Related ideas...   20   22   33   60

Confidence with visitors

A well-trained dog will greet visitors in a friendly manner, with four paws on the ground, before settling down quietly, leaving you to entertain your guests in peace. Many dogs, however, are a little too enthusiastic with their meet and greets, and may be clumsy and persistently pushy.

Anxious or overexcited dogs may growl and bark threateningly when guests arrive, or nip and herd visitors when they try to leave. Unless you want to spend the rest of your life friendless and alone, you need to help your dog to learn self-control.

Of course, one option is to keep him shut away, but his stress levels are likely to be the same and will affect other areas of his life. It is far more rewarding to teach your bouncy dog an appropriate greeting exercise (see page 51) and to settle in his bed or a mat on cue before your next guests arrive. If he is timid, work through the exercises for timidity (see page 50).

TTouches

- Ear Slides
- Slow, connected TTouches through the whole body
- Tail Work
- Mouth Work
- Python Lifts down shoulders
- Clouded Leopard TTouches around the chest and hindquarters

Safe area

Meanwhile, create a safe area where he can stay until you have his behaviour under control. Stair gates, crates, and closed doors can all be valuable management tools, and you may need to keep the dog away from the entrance so that visitors can come in and sit down comfortably before you bring him into the room on a lead. If he tends to pull towards them, try using a harness or balance-lead to avoid excess pressure on his collar as this may restrict his airway, increasing anxious or excitable behaviour. You may also find a body-wrap or doggy T-shirt helpful.

Encourage him to settle using some calming TTouches and keep calm and relaxed so that your dog can follow your example. Once your dog is under control your visitors will also be able to relax, which in turn will reassure your dog.

Case History

MONTY

Our work with Monty featured in *100 Ways to Train the Perfect Dog*, as Jo was experiencing all sorts of problems with her charming dog. He had lived in several homes before he was adopted by Jo, and was deeply suspicious of and threatened by new people. When visitors called, Jo would have to take him from the room, but this did not help Monty grow in confidence. Working with TTouches and teaching him to settle in his bed on cue transformed Monty, and he has increased his circle of friends as a result. He really loves attention from other people if he trusts them, and it has been a pleasure to watch the world open up for him and Jo.

TIP

Don't let well-meaning visitors pursue your dog around trying to force him to make friends. This is the quickest way to teach an anxious dog to defend himself.

USEFUL GROUND WORK EXERCISES

Different surfaces

Raised boards

Pick up sticks

Labyrinth

Monty is now accepting of visitors to his house.

Related ideas...   33   55   60   63   71

Calming overexcitement

Many dogs live in a permanent state of stress and/or excitability and need to learn that relaxation is also an option. Make sure that your dog has plenty of outlets for his energy, but remember to teach him to how to calm down as well. TTouch body work and ground work are ideal for helping dogs to learn self-control.

Wearing a body-wrap helps the majority of dogs to calm, and if a dog is relaxed he will remember all the other appropriate behaviours you are teaching him. If your dog goes nuts when you put on the wrap, quietly take it off and try again a few minutes later.

In 15 years of TTouch work we have only come across a couple of dogs that did not like the wrap, and it is a cheap and pretty effortless way of helping your dog to settle. You can use it at home or when you are out and about, but if you are worried that people will think your dog has been in an accident, use a doggy T-shirt instead.

Ground work

If contact is over-stimulating for your dog, start with ground work using a harness and a double-clipped lead. Use your clicker to teach him to sit or stand at intervals through the ground work exercises. Encourage him to use his nose and drop some treats on the ground through the Labyrinth. Try a face-wrap if he loses focus.

Give him time to run around off the lead and then quietly finish the session with a walk through the Labyrinth and a relaxing TTouch body work session.

TTouch work will help you to find areas of tension that may be contributing to your dog's excitement. It is a valuable tool to help you to instil some calm.

Woody is now really relaxing and his face is less worried.

Woody is a very excitable Labrador but he actually has worry lines over his eyes.

TTouches

- *Ear Slides*

- *Chimp and Llama TTouches around the head and muzzle*

- *Tail Work*

- *Slow Springboks*

- *Smooth, connected Zigzags through the body*

- *Clouded Leopard TTouches around the chest*

- *Python Lifts down shoulders and front limbs*

USEFUL GROUND WORK EXERCISES

Labyrinth

Fan

Raised poles

Pick up sticks

Different surfaces

Related ideas...   47   48   63   70

Compulsive shadow chasing

61

This behaviour can be a real problem for both owner and dog, but a combination of clicker work, TTouches, ground work and patience can produce some outstanding results, as this case study shows. The TTouch head-wrap can be hugely beneficial when dealing with compulsive behaviour.

We tend to see shadow and/or light chasing more commonly in Springer spaniels and Collies. Dogs can develop this habit due to lack of appropriate exercise and stimulation, and it may also be linked to an over refined herding gene. Teaching the dog alternative behaviours to encourage them to focus and use their brain appropriately is paramount, and a combination of clicker training and TTouch can go a long way to reducing this problem.

Getting to work

The earlier you can start to work with your dog the better, as this behaviour can quickly escalate. Unfortunately it may have been encouraged in his early life, as many people find it cute or funny, and may have even teased the dog with reflected light from watches and so on. As the dog can never catch the shadow or the light his actions remain unrewarded and the dog can quickly become obsessed.

Teaching him to play a shared game, to retrieve and to search for hidden food and toys will give him a more appropriate outlet, but you will have to do your homework to find something that motivates your dog to play. Patience is the key and, in our opinion, groundwork is a must. The head wrap, body wrap and leg wraps can be of great benefit for dogs that have compulsive behaviours. Slow movement through the ground work obstacles can help to trigger the feel good factor and give him a new and calmer experience in what may be a highly stimulating situation.

At home

Start working at home, and if you have to beg, borrow or steal a large gazebo to diffuse shadows and light over a labyrinth do so, although personally we have never had to go to these lengths. Keep the sessions short and repeat them throughout the day, interspersing the ground work exercises with TTouch work. Practice the 'look at me' exercise (see page 28) so that you can start teaching him that it is more rewarding for him to focus on you than lights or shadows. Use TTouch work to help him settle in the home, and bear in mind that he may have problems with his eyesight and may need to be checked over by a vet.

Combining body work and ground work helps to keep the sessions varied.

Ground work such as the Labyrinth helps to improve focus. This little spaniel is usually very distracted when out and we use the same exercises and equipment when working with dogs that are aroused by moving light or shadows.

Related ideas...   12   32   58

62

The vacuum cleaner

Dogs may chase vacuum cleaners (or lawn mowers) because they see them as moving toys, but it might also be because they find the noise unsettling. All equipment of this kind is potentially dangerous to your dog so it is important to teach him to behave appropriately.

Some dogs may have been chased with a vacuum cleaner in an attempt to stop their early 'play' behaviours but this may not always be the case. If your dog reacts the moment he sees the vacuum cleaner you may find it helpful to start with the machine outside to change his expectations. The aim is to teach the dog to be calm and to feel safe around the machine but in order to overcome this problem you will need to break the exercise down into simple steps.

Put the machine in a room or in the yard and then fetch your dog. Use a harness and a double clipped lead so that you do not inadvertently pull on his neck. Keep him well away from the machine and drop some treats on the floor. Click as he starts to move towards them. Walk him nearer the machine, around it and past it clicking and treating any calm behaviour. Pay attention to his posture and use the TTouches to keep him relaxed. If at any point he becomes aroused, walk him quietly away and click and treat him the moment he shifts his focus away from the vacuum cleaner. Keep the session short.

Once he is calm in the presence of the machine enlist the help of a friend and ask them to stand near it while you click and treat your calm and confident dog and repeat the early steps, walking around the vacuum, past it and so on. Remember to use your TTouches and do not forget to use treats and verbal praise. Walk your dog quietly away for a moment and ask your friend to first handle, then gently move the machine. If at any point your dog becomes aroused go back a few steps and repeat the earlier exercises.

When he is able to stay calm near the moving machine, you may need to get him accustomed to the noise in a separate exercise. This will involve him hearing the engine without actually seeing the vacuum moving, so you can ask someone to switch it on for a few seconds in another room while you do TTouch work and click and treat all calm behaviours. Build up the length of time that the machine is on over several sessions if necessary. You can also try using groundwork (if you have the space) as this allows him to move but in a calm controlled way. Continue to build on these steps by teaching him to be calm around the machine while it is on in his presence but not moving and then ask a friend to handle, slowly move it around and so on. Remember you can go back a few steps at any point.

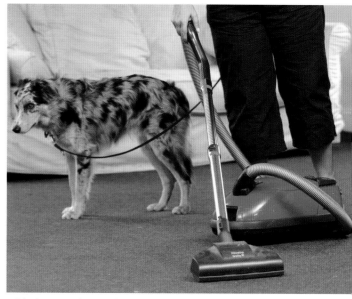

Mikka is stressed even when the vacuum cleaner is not switched on.

Mikka is progressing through the program, gradually getting used to the movement of the vacuum without reacting.

TTouches

- *Ear Slides*
- *Racoon TTouches around the shoulder blades*
- *Back Lifts*
- *Connected TTouches along the back*

Related ideas... 82 83 85 86

Jumping up

Jumping up is a natural greeting for most dogs, but while it is appealing in a puppy it becomes a problem as the dog matures. Not everyone likes dogs and not many people relish the idea of a fancy paw print pattern on clean trousers or skirts. Teach your dog a more acceptable alternative behaviour using the clicker.

Jumping up can be endearing in a puppy but quickly becomes a nuisance as the dog matures.

Shouting at a dog may encourage him to jump more as he frantically tries to appease you. Instead, ignore any jumping up by standing in a neutral position with your arms crossed. The moment your dog backs off and/or sits, click and drop a treat to the floor. Repeat this several times until he nderstands that he gets more attention and a yummy reward if he keeps his feet on the floor.

Enlist the help of a friend to build on this exercise. Call the dog and reward his calm behaviour, then ask your friend to do the same. This is a fun game for most dogs.

Practise doing TTouch work with him when he is already quiet so that he learns how good it makes him feel. Dogs remember TTouch work very quickly, and a few Ear Slides or slow circular TTouches can help him to regain self-control more quickly next time he is aroused.

TIP

Pop a half-wrap or doggy T-shirt on your dog to give him better body-awareness and to help him stay calm.

We taught Woody to sit and give his paw. A body-wrap and a house-line will help calm and contain the dog while working on the new behaviour. Build on it so that your dog is able to greet everyone in a more appropriate way.

TTouches

- *Python Lifts down both shoulders and front legs simultaneously*

- *Ear Slides*

- *Slow Springboks over his body*

- *Troika TTouch*

Related ideas...   **45**   **48**   **60**

64 Escaping

If you own Houndini, you are going to have to be as creative as your friend. Escapologists are usually bored and have discovered that there is more merriment to be had down the road, hunting for squirrels or cats or raiding your neighbour's rubbish. Some dogs may be scared or have a bad association with the garden.

Your unfaithful friend may be leaving you because he loves to chase or scavenge, for example, or because he hates to be alone. Whatever the reason, it is wholly our responsibility to keep our dogs mentally and physically stimulated, content and above all, safe. If you know the reason why he keeps scarpering, then work through the appropriate exercise in this book and *100 Ways to Train the Perfect Dog*.

It goes without saying that you need to ensure all your boundaries are secure. Dogs can be skilled contortionists if the motivation to escape is high. They can squeeze under gates or through spiky hedges, and they can undo latches and run along narrow walls.

It is unfair to expect an intelligent or working dog to loaf around all day in a dull environment, so daily exercise is paramount. Teach him tricks and games to help him to use his brain and bond with you. Interact with him both indoors and out, and incorporate some slow movements into the garden activities so that he learns to settle there. If all your games are noisy and fun he will feel bereft if you nip back indoors. Use TTouches to give him a pleasant experience in his garden. Avoid sticking to a routine: if he knows you will only play with him in the afternoon, the thought of an early morning stroll will still appeal.

Keep some special toys for outside play – if he has constant access to them indoors their novelty will quickly wear off. Gnawing calms dogs down and encourages them to settle in one place, so provide plenty of appropriate things to gnaw on. Make sure he has access to fresh water and a covered place to hide and/or rest.

Enrich the garden

Hide some toys and treats, and teach your dog how to search, so that rewards come from being on his own property. Some dogs love to play with water, drag or throw things around, and others may love to dig. You can build him his very own playground, with low climbing frames, paddling pools, tunnels, steps, ramps and other hiding places made from wood, plastic sand boxes and old tyres. Even a humble cardboard box will be highly prized by many dogs. Obviously any construction needs to be safe, with no sharp edges or splinters to cause injury.

Cookie Dough Dynamo has her very own climbing-frame, with a ball pit under a raised platform accessed by a ramp or stairs. You do not need to go to these lengths but you do need to teach your dog that good things happen in the garden.

TTouches

- *Mouth Work*
- *Python Lifts along the back and down legs*
- *TTouches around the hindquarters*
- *Raccoon TTouches around the shoulders and withers*

Related ideas...   20   25   79   81   82   83   92

Destroying the garden

Destructive behaviour in the garden is usually the sign of a bored or worried dog. He does not know that you spent hours toiling to plant those lovely little flowers that are now scattered across your lawn and stuck between his teeth. All he knows is that shredding them was jolly good fun.

If your dog really enjoys working things out, you could make him his own 'dog tree', which you can fill with fun things. Use the clicker to teach him how to pull treat-filled plastic bottles or toys from the tree.

If you are unable to spend time playing with and teaching your dog, you must expect him to make up his own entertainment. If he is destructive in the garden it is likely that he also runs amok indoors. The first step is to teach an 'off' or 'leave' cue in a quiet, controlled environment so that you can stop what he is doing and re-direct him to a more appropriate doggy toy. Stay neutral if he regresses; remember, your attention (even if you are furious) is better than no attention at all. Make a note to spend more time with him in future.

Alternative entertainment

Play with him using one of the interactive Nina Ottosson games that teach your dog to use his mouth to slide and lift blocks from the board to access hidden treats. This will give him a more satisfying and rewarding outlet for his skills than a wilting pansy ever can. And buy him an indestructible toy such as a Boomer Ball that he can have fun chasing and playing with.

Use your TTouches to teach him that he can also relax in the garden.

TTouches

- *Mouth Work*
- *Chimp and Llama TTouches around the muzzle*
- *Tail Work*
- *Slow, connected Clouded Leopard TTouches all over the body*

Related ideas...   21   43   64   80

Digging

Digging is a natural behaviour but is also a sign of a bored or stressed dog. Follow all the advice in the other sections, but if your dog still persists with his journey to the centre of the earth, build him his own digging pit.

You can construct a pit out of lengths of wood, or purchase a raised bed frame from a garden supplier. You can also build a simple one by digging a small area of garden and hiding things in it. Some garden mulches are highly toxic to dogs, so stick to soil. Teach your dog to search for hidden toys or treats, as shown in *100 Ways to Train the Perfect Dog*, then bury some in his pit and hide others under flowerpots that can be placed on top of the soil.

USEFUL GROUND WORK EXERCISES

Labyrinth

Fan

Pick up sticks

Teeter totter

TIP

If you do not want soil liberally scattered around, put some large plastic dog balls in the pit so that he has to use his paws to move them around in order to find the treats.

Related ideas...   20   64   65

67 Excessive barking

If your dog barks a lot when he is outside, you need to establish if he is bored, cold, aroused by the noise of passing people and animals or concerned about being on his own. Dogs love to be part of the social scene and many dislike being shut into the garden for long periods of time.

If your dog spends a long time alone in the garden it is understandable that he will want to protest. It is important that you spend time stimulating him in an appropriate way so that he is able to settle on his own. You should also try to enrich his outdoor environment in any way that you can, following the tips given elsewhere in this section, so that he is not bored. Provide somewhere comfortable in the garden where he can hide and rest.

The techniques and TTouches to follow are largely the same as those used to stop excessive barking in the home (see page 38). Try teaching your dog to bark on cue with the clicker and then teaching a 'quiet' cue.

Give your dog a TTouch session in the garden, or start in the house if he is more likely to settle indoors.

Teach your dog to walk calmly on the lead and ensure that he has plenty of exercise.

The calming band can be used to give your dog the experience of being calm and settled in the garden.

USEFUL GROUND WORK EXERCISES

Labyrinth

Fan

Weave cones

TTouches

- Ear Slides
- Raccoon TTouches around the back of the neck
- Lying Leopard TTouches over the top of the head
- Clouded Leopard TTouches either side of the temples and across the forehead
- Tail Slides
- Lying Leopard and Clouded Leopard TTouches all over the body

Related ideas...   22   64   65   70

Brooms and rakes

Many dogs see brooms and rakes as huge interactive toys, and play is often encouraged in puppies because it looks cute. Owners soon stop laughing when the dog matures, and attempts to sweep or rake result in a wrestling match. If this behaviour becomes established your dog will become very excited as soon as he catches sight of these items.

When a dog becomes highly aroused and loses control he may redirect and bite a nearby hand or leg without being aware of his actions and with no real intention of malice. The best way to teach him to be calm around a broom or a rake is to break the lesson down into small steps. He is likely to become excited as soon as his 'toy' appears, so be prepared.

The first small step is to lay the article in the garden. Bring your dog out and let him see you scatter some small, very tasty treats on the ground at an appropriate distance from it. You want to start working at a distance where your dog remains calm. Click as he approaches the treats. There is no need to do a prolonged session. Short, calm, successful sessions where he does not become aroused will be far more beneficial.

Helping to retain self-control

TTouch and a body-wrap may help him to retain some self-control, and he should be contained on a lead or house-line, preferably attached to a harness. The line can be held or left dragging and is there so that you can safely lead him away if he becomes too excited.

Progress to having another person standing by the article, then touching it, holding it upright, beginning to move it, moving it more vigorously and so on. Use your clicker, rewards and TTouches to teach your dog that it is far more rewarding to stay calm. Take your time, moving back a step if necessary. To build a solid foundation for change, your dog should be able to remain consistently calm at all times and in different places around the broom or rake.

You can use brooms as part of the labyrinth or walk-over poles to shift his focus as his behaviour improves.

Realistically, you may still need to sweep or rake while you are working on the problem behaviour, so put the dog in another area with a stuffed Kong or bone to occupy him to avoid reinforcing any inappropriate interaction.

Leo is rewarded for his beautiful behaviour and the clicker is a fun and rewarding way of engaging his teenage brain!

Leo is learning how to stay calm and controlled around a moving broom.

TTouches

- *Ear Slides*
- *Racoon TTouches around the shoulder blades*
- *Back Lifts*
- *Connected TTouches along the back*

IN THE GARDEN

Related ideas...   12   42   80   81   82   85

Hot air balloons

Hot air balloons are both noisy and visually stimulating for dogs. They move slowly, and not many dogs will have had enough exposure to them to learn that they are not a threat. Even if you cannot totally allay your dog's fears, you can prevent his stress levels from increasing with every balloon he sees.

Teach your dog to walk under obstacles such as through a tent or under a shower curtain. Many dogs that are afraid of balloons are worried about walking under new things. They are often also spooked by plastic bags. Try working through the exercise for fear of the hose (see page 93), using plastic bags instead of lengths of hosepipe, but make sure they are securely fixed so they don't flap.

Use a doggy T-shirt or half-wrap to give the dog a sense of security and do some gentle Ear Slides to help lower his heart rate and respiration. Accustom him to being stroked with a wand to give him greater connection through his body and to get used to things passing over his head.

Be creative

Teach him some simple ground work exercises and gradually introduce new shapes into the ground work area. The more experiences you can give your dog in a quiet, controlled environment the better he will be able to adapt to new situations.

If a balloon does appear and he starts to get upset, stay calm and use the TTouches to settle him.

Teach him a 'Leave' cue and practice his recall and hand follow (see page 102 and *100 Ways to Train the Perfect Dog*), so that you can regain his focus, and gently lead him inside if he starts fixating on the balloon.

TTouches

- *Ear Slides*
- *Tail Work*
- *Connected TTouches over the whole body*
- *Python Lifts down all four legs*
- *Clouded Leopard TTouches around the chest and hindquarters*
- *Zigzags*

USEFUL GROUND WORK EXERCISES

Labyrinth, gradually introducing new objects

Raised board

Teeter totter

Different surfaces

Sally is really concerned about hot air balloons which often appear over the horizon at Tilley Farm. Tina uses a T-shirt to help Sally feel a little more secure and makes a safe place for her where she can hide.

TTouches around the muzzle combined with Ear Work can be useful for dogs that are overly emotional or afraid.

Related ideas...　72　80

Passers-by

While it is natural for dogs to protect their territory, a dog that is constantly running along the fence barking at every passer-by will be extremely stressed. Dogs that are tight in the back and neck can become more aroused, and a constant state of stress will contribute to tension in these areas.

TTouch work and management are a key part in reducing this behaviour. Most dogs respond well if the visual stimulus is reduced, so explore your fencing options and invest in some panelling if necessary. Avoid leaving your dog unattended in the garden where possible: someone may be teasing him.

Enrich the garden (see page 86) so that passers-by are not the sole source of interest, and teach your dog a good recall and 'Leave' cue so that you can call him away. You can also set up some ground work in the garden and work with him in a calm, controlled manner so that he learns to have a different association as people pass by.

IN THE GARDEN

USEFUL GROUND WORK EXERCISES

Raised poles

Labyrinth

TTouches

- *Ear Slides*
- *Clouded Leopard TTouches around the hindquarters*
- *Belly Lifts with wrap*
- *Raccoon and/or Clouded Leopard TTouches down either side of the spine*

TIP

Cover a gate or fencing with panels to reduce your dog's visibility of passers by.

If your dog is aroused by people passing by, an open boundary like this will increase his anxiety.

Related ideas...   59   60   81

71 Guarding

Knowing that our dogs will deter burglars gives us confidence, and appropriate barking to alert us to visitors arriving can be helpful. However, if a dog's natural guarding instincts are in overdrive, trouble may lie ahead. You may be giving him conflicting advice, encouraging him to bark to ward off intruders but to remain quiet when the papers are delivered.

Dogs tend to guard at any point of entry, whether it's a gate, over a fence, a gap in the hedge, or through doors and windows. The fact that your dog may have met a person before is no guarantee that he will not challenge them in these circumstances, especially if you are not around. We are required by law to ensure the safety of anyone who enters our property and it is our responsibility to make sure that visitors don't have to come face to face with a guarding dog. Consider putting your mailbox and bell on the other side of your front entrance so that visitors can alert you to their prescence.

Teach your dog a good recall (see page 102) and work through some of the other exercises in *100 Ways to Train the Perfect Dog*. A dog that is poorly socialized and left to his own devices is more likely to display defensive behaviours than one that is well trained and confident.

If your dog guards your property you need to ensure that he does not have access to points of entry.

You should also teach an appropriate behaviour for when callers come to the house. Teaching the dog to sit on a target such as a mat means unknown callers can still be aware of his presence but keeps your dog under control (see page 63). Place the mat at a safe distance from the door. Using a clicker, train your dog to target the mat and settle down, then gradually shape his behaviour so that he will target the mat when you are standing by the door. Go back to standing nearer to your dog and his mat, then add the distraction of a person knocking at the door or ringing the bell.

Guarding issues are increased in dogs that do not have other outlets for their energy, so good training, games and exercise are key to reducing stress levels.

USEFUL GROUND WORK EXERCISES

Raised poles

Labyrinth

TTouches

- *Ear Slides*
- *Raccoon TTouches either side of head*
- *Clouded Leopard TTouches around the neck, back and hindquarters*
- *Tail Work*

Related ideas...   44   60

Fear of the hose

Dogs may develop a fear of hosepipes if they have spent time in puppy farms or shelters where hoses were used to clean down runs while they were in them, or if they have been deliberately sprayed with water as a punishment. You can use ground work to overcome this problem in small easy steps.

Teach your dog to negotiate the labyrinth and/or some walk-over poles (see page 24). When he walks into the labyrinth and/or over the poles, click and drop a treat to the ground, and repeat the click and treat as he moves through and/or over the poles.

When he can negotiate the course with ease and is confident, cut some long lengths of old hosepipe and lay these strips next to the walk-over or labyrinth poles one at a time. Build on this exercise slowly, backing up his confidence with the clicker and some treats.

Once you have laid the hosepipe pieces alongside every pole, begin to remove the poles one at a time. You may have to spread this exercise out over a couple of sessions if your dog loses focus or tires. Keep removing the poles until he is walking around and/or over the hosepipe.

Incorporate any object that your dog is fearful of into ground work exercises – hoses make great labyrinths but you can adapt the idea to address other concerns.

The next steps

Set up the exercise in different areas in your garden. You can also stroke him with a wand as shown in the fear of contact exercise (see page 72). When he is happy with that, slide the wand through a length of hose and repeat the stroking. Build up his confidence to the point where you can stroke him with the hosepipe.

The final step is to set up the ground work near a water supply and run another length of hosepipe from the tap to near the ground work. Make sure the new hose is the same colour as the one you have been using, and incorporate the new hose into the exercise. For example, you could lead the dog over the cut lengths and then over the full length of hose, or through the labyrinth and then over the hose. Turn on the tap a little so that a slow flow of water trickles out of the hose and repeat the exercise.

You do not need your dog to become so confident that he wants to play with the water (although this may happen). Your aim is simply to stop him panicking the moment he spots the hose. You can try introducing your dog to the delights of water play with a romp on a beach or through a stream.

Use TTouch work to help your dog to feel calmer around the scary hose.

TTouches

- *Ear Slides*

- *Clouded Leopard TTouches around his hindquarters*

- *Python Lifts down all four legs*

- *Stroking him all over with the wand*

USEFUL GROUND WORK EXERCISES

Different surfaces

Raised poles

Labyrinth

Related ideas...   33   99

73 Mugging strangers

Your dog may have got the idea that he has every right to conduct a full body search for treats, or demand cuddles from everybody he meets while you are out walking. Not every one will appreciate this. It is far more appropriate to teach your dog the polite way to greet people when out and about.

Train your dog to greet you by touching the back of your hand with his nose, as described in *100 Ways to Train the Perfect Dog*, and discourage other people from touching your dog unless he has been offered the hand-touch greeting and remained calm.

Kind-hearted people who insist on giving a treat to every dog they meet encourage mugging behaviour. To try to pre-empt and discourage this, make sure your dog knows where his treats come from by using a recognizable treat bag, and hand this to the other person to use. The aim is for your dog to learn that there is no point in begging for food from others unless he actually sees his treat bag changing hands.

Some dogs are just so delighted to see people that they dive at them and demand a fuss. If your dog is like this, keep him on a lead or long line until you have taught a red-hot recall (see page 102). If he is likely to head off towards a dot-sized figure on the horizon you will also find it useful to train the chase recall described in *100 Ways to Train the Perfect Dog*. Work out the distance at which your dog begins to react to people, remembering this may vary depending on location and circumstances.

TTouch and ground work

Explore TTouch body work at home and find the touches that calm him quickly so that they can be used if your dog becomes overexcited while out and about. Ground work exercises will help your dog to be more aware of his movement and encourage him to shift his focus. Use a double

Pilot's greeting behaviour is rather spectacular, but not very appropriate. He behaves the same way with other dogs.

connection such as a harness and collar to help him to move slowly and in balance. A body-wrap or T-shirt may help your dog to be more self-controlled. Face or head-wraps can also be helpful.

Pilot begins to learn that Sarah is the treat dispenser and sits calmly next to Ryan and the other dog.

TTouches

• *Ear Slides*
• *Slow Springbok*
• *Troika*
• *Tail Work*
• *Connected circular TTouches over the body*

USEFUL GROUND WORK EXERCISES

Teeter totter
Raised boards
Different surfaces
Uneven poles
Weave cones
Labyrinth

Related ideas...   60   63   76

94

Pulling on the lead

Teaching a dog to walk calmly by your side will enable you to help him with other problems, such as fear of cars or reactive behaviours towards other dogs. There are several ways to teach a dog to walk in balance on the lead and ground work plays an important role, encouraging him to become more thoughtful in his movement.

The way you attach the lead can make a quick and dramatic difference. Experiment to see which is going to be most successful for you and your dog. As it takes two to maintain a pull, think about your own posture and balance: bracing through your own body will trigger the same response in your dog. Sometimes we remove the lead altogether and work with a long rope threaded through the harness D-rings to take the pressure off the collar, as this can trigger a habitual pulling response.

Walking a dog on a harness with only one attachment can trigger more of a pull, and it is well worth investing in a TTouch harness and a double-clipped lead if you are struggling to keep your lively hound under control. Try clipping one end to the front ring and the other to a ring on the back. Ask your dog to steady and slow down his movement with a gentle 'ask and release' on the front ring (see page 25). To help him stay in balance, you want him to walk with his shoulder parallel to your leg. If he is walking ahead of you he is more likely to lunge and pull.

Work over poles and through the labyrinth to improve his concentration and mark his beautiful balanced movement with your clicker and some rewards. Intersperse the ground work with body work, as we have found this helps dogs to learn more quickly and to retain more information. Many dogs are disconnected through their hindquarters, which adds to the problem. Using the TTouches listed will increase mind/body-awareness.

Olle, this lovely young boxer cross, is very powerful and has little self-control when on the lead.

TTouches

- *Zigzags*
- *Slow, connected Clouded Leopard TTouches along the body*
- *Tail Work*
- *Leg Circles*
- *Light slow Springbok TTouches over the body*

USEFUL GROUND WORK EXERCISES

Raised poles

Fan

Labyrinth

Balance-lead

Balance-lead plus

Sliding line

Use a harness, a double-clipped lead, a clicker and some treats to teach your dog how to walk around patterns of poles.

Related ideas... 14 15 16 60 75 78

75 Spinning and twisting on the lead

Some dogs spin so badly that they are unable to walk on the lead. TTouch ground work and body work have proved extremely successful with dogs that have this behaviour, and all the exercises will benefit your dog.

Make a 'double diamond' harness as shown in the pictures using a long, soft flat training lead or a soft length of rope (see page 26). The aim is to be able to influence the dog's body, as opposed to stopping the spinning by holding on for dear life. If possible, enlist the help of a friend who can support the dog on the other side.

Mark any calming in his behaviour with a click and treat. Keep the sessions really short – initially we look for only one or two steps forward if we are working with a dog that has a chronic problem. As the dog's behaviour improves, use a half-wrap to give him better body-awareness.

Pilot is quite a contortionist when it comes to walking on the lead.

She also uses TTouch work to help improve his body-awareness.

She then progresses to a half-wrap and uses treats to reinforce Pilot's calming behaviour.

TTouches

- *Connected circular TTouches from head to hindquarters*
- *Tail Work*
- *Leg Circles*
- *Lying Leopard TTouches and Lifts along ribs and back*
- *Slow Springbok TTouches all over the body*
- *Mouth Work*
- *Ear Slides*

USEFUL GROUND WORK EXERCISES

Labyrinth

Weave cones

Walk-over poles

Different surfaces

Sarah uses a double diamond to encourage Pilot to move in a straight line.

Related ideas...   15   16   74   76

96

Leaping and lunging

Some dogs have never learnt to walk on a lead, and others are so overwhelmed by the outside world that they forget any training they may have had and lunge and leap their way down the street.

Olle not only pulls on the lead, he leaps, spins and grabs as well.

Working down the limbs helps to ground him and encourages him to think about his feet.

TTouches

- *Clouded Leopard TTouches around the chest*
- *Python Lifts down the legs*
- *Ear Slides*
- *Chimp TTouches around the muzzle*
- *Mouth Work*
- *Tail Work*
- *Raccoon TTouches around the hip joints*

Before you put your dog on the lead, use TTouches to calm and show him the possibility of relaxation. Introduce him to the half-wrap. Invest in a TTouch harness and a double-clipped lead, and attach one clip to the front ring and the other to a D-ring on the back. If he still leaps about with this two-point contact, try the sliding line (see page 25).

Ground work

Set up some ground work at home where there are fewer distractions. Working over poles will encourage your dog to think about his feet. Keep the lead neutral, making sure you have plenty of slack in it, and avoid bracing in your own body. This will help to prevent you inadvertently triggering more out of control behaviour and also protect your back and shoulders if he does leap forward.

Give the dog an 'ask and release' signal on the front ring (see page 25) and try to keep his shoulder in line with your leg. Mark any normal steps with a click and treat if you can, or get a friend to watch and click while you treat.

Keep the sessions short. Even if you end the first session with the dog still leaping around you may notice a huge difference when you start the second. Sarah worked with a four-year-old dog that was handed in to the Dogs' Trust in Merseyside. He lunged and leapt so badly that the staff had never seen him actually walk in balance on the lead. He was also reactive when he saw another dog, but by the second session he was walking calmly on a loose lead through the labyrinth, and was able to stand quietly watching other dogs.

USEFUL GROUND WORK EXERCISES

Raised and uneven poles

Labyrinth

Fan

Different surfaces

Although he still leaps around when on the sliding line, he quickly settles with this new experience.

77 Agoraphobia

Fear of being outside is relatively common in dogs. The vet should be your first port of call to rule out medical problems such as joint pain, muscle weakness or ear infections. Once your dog has been given a clean bill of health you can work through some of the tips below.

If a dog experiences success he will grow in confidence. Set up some ground work in the garden or in your home to give him a new experience in a familiar environment, and use a half-wrap or doggy T-shirt to help him feel more secure. Use a harness with a double-clipped lead attached to the front and back. Removing the lead from the collar can help the dog to feel more secure about moving forwards.

Starting wherever your dog is comfortable, sit or stand next to him and stroke his ears to lower his heart rate and respiration. Face in the direction you want to move, and avoid standing over your dog or staring at him. Gently stroke the lead and as he steps forward click and drop a treat. You can also try dropping a treat a few paces in front and, as he moves forward to take it, click the clicker. If he freezes and is too worried to eat, gently and slowly circle his legs and rock his withers.

Do not rush him in any way. Most people find that the body-wrap and a few TTouches can give their dogs new confidence in one session, but others may need more time. Be patient and, when you are ready to progress further, try to pre-empt the point of freeze or panic and turn for home. Be prepared to vary the distance you go; if you set your sights on a four-hour hike your dog will pick up on your thoughts and feel overwhelmed.

Ground work at home in a safe environment is the perfect step for preparing your dog for the great outdoors.

USEFUL GROUND WORK EXERCISES

Raised boards

Labyrinth

A confident friend can also help timid dogs to be less concerned

TTouches

- Ear Slides
- Clouded Leopard TTouches around hindquarters
- Leg circles
- Zigzags
- Wither rocking

Related ideas... 33   78

Walking on the lead

This may be linked to agoraphobia or it may be that the dog has never been asked to walk in balance before and is panicked by the containment. Learning to walk with the lead on a harness is certainly more pleasant for most dogs and will give you better control over your dog if he struggles to escape.

It goes without saying that you will need to practise at home and it can be easier for your dog if you incorporate lead walking into something he has already learnt. Teach him to walk through and over a variety of low-level obstacles using any of the ground work exercises. Use a half-wrap or T-shirt to help him focus.

Enlist the help of a friend and use a sliding line through the D-rings of the harness to give the dog a sense of being contained on a lead while walking without overloading him.

Once he has settled, attach a double-clipped lead to the back of the harness and repeat the exercises, over several sessions if necessary. When your dog is confident attach the second clip to the front of the harness.

Make sure the line is neutral and pay attention to your own posture. If you grip the lead and try to manoeuvre the dog with your own body weight he is more likely to panic and leap around or freeze.

A body-wrap and some body work, at first using a paint-brush and a fake hand, helped her to gain confidence.

This little poodle became very agitated when on the lead and was also reactive to being touched.

TTouches

- *Clouded Leopard TTouches around the chest*
- *Python Lifts*
- *Leg Circles*
- *Wither Rocking*
- *Tail Work*
- *Belly Lifts*

TIP

If you teach your dog to target and follow your hand, as shown in *100 Ways to Train the Perfect Dog*, you can use this while he is walking by your side to gain his attention if he becomes distracted.

Related ideas...   15   74   75   76   77

79 Reactive behaviours towards other dogs

The majority of dogs that show reactive behaviours to other dogs are likely to have had bad experiences with another dog at some point in their lives. Puppyhood encounters can also lead to a dog that develops fearful behaviours towards other dogs. In some cases, it may simply be that the dog was not socialised early in life.

Whatever the reason behind your dog's behaviour, it is important to recognise that most reactive behaviours stem from a place of fear.

There is a lot that you can do as the owner of a dog that has issues with other dogs, but it would also be practical for you to work with a trainer on a one-to-one basis who can teach you kind, positive techniques that will help your dog to develop confidence and self-control. Avoid anyone who recommends hitting your dog, giving him an electric shock, tying him to a tree whilst other dogs are marched past him or using noise aversion and so on, as these techniques are unpleasant. They are also more likely to increase his stress levels and, in turn, escalate his reactive behaviours.

Teach your dog to wear a muzzle and also encourage him to look at you when you call his name. We use the clicker in situations such as these to mark any calming in his behaviour or relaxing in his posture, rather than just for getting his attention. If you are unsure about your clicker skills, find a trainer who can help you.

Mattie has overcome many issues but is still concerned by the presence of other dogs. Imogen teaches her to negotiate the ground work exercises in a calm environment.

Tina brings in a fake dog to assess how the dog (the real one!) is likely to respond, and Imogen rewards Mattie's calm behaviour.

Marie keeps the calm Charlie Brown at a distance that is acceptable for Mattie, and Tina and Imogen continue with the ground work.

When Charlie Brown starts walking, Mattie kicks off.

Tina and Imogen remain calm and do some TTouches on Mattie.

Mattie remains beautifully focused even though Charlie is directly in her eyeline.

Case History

JASPER

Jasper is a 2½-year-old Rottweiler, rescued because his owners felt they needed a dog to protect their home. When they met him for the first time, he sniffed around the room, found where the treats were hidden and lay down in front of them for a belly rub and fuss. Once in his new home, however, he jumped up at strangers, stole and chewed things, pulled on the lead, nipped his owners and barked at everything when in the car. He barked, howled and lunged at other dogs and on one occasion dragged his owner across a road on her back.

His owners called in behaviourists and trainers but were shown aversive techniques that only made the situation worse. They feared that they had failed, but then stumbled upon TTouch and Marie's website, where they found lots of useful information and hope. They booked an appointment. Marie came up with effective ways to help modify Jasper's reactive behaviour, and his owners started clicker training and TTouch, getting Jasper used to a life-sized fake dog and reinforcing his good behaviour.

Very gradually, Jasper is becoming much calmer. He no longer jumps at strangers, lies down in the car, does not pull on the lead and follows clicker commands like a seasoned pro. He is now able to ignore other dogs if cheese is on offer. His owners love TTouch and are looking forward to rescuing their second dog and sharing their love and new improved training techniques.

Related ideas...   25   50

80

Good recall

It is a misconception that certain breeds of dog can never learn a solid recall, though it is true that those bred to think and work away from people are more independent. The key to a good recall is to find which rewards motivate the dog and use them efficiently. Avoid taking short cuts and do not rush the training.

A dog may perform a perfect recall in training class but appear deaf when called to return at the local park. He is not simply being disobedient. Unless his training is fitted into everyday life and the recall practised in different situations and locations, he will not truly understand that it means 'Stop what you are doing, come directly to me and wait to be released again or have your lead put on.'

A good recall means that you can let your dog off the lead safely, so it is important. To be effective it needs to be rewarding for your dog, so once you have taught the basic exercise, introduce changes. Recall lots of times, varying the reward. Sometimes clip his lead on and walk a little way, or use a little Ear Work and Clouded Leopard TTouches so that he stays with you, then release him again. Recalls should offer the potential of a game, a fuss, treats and more freedom, not just the the end of the walk.

Use your TTouches to increase his body-awareness and to improve concentration and focus. Dogs with a poor recall are often tight through the muzzle and hindquarters. Use the ground work to teach your dog to watch you and to help him move in balance.

Sight and scent can have a powerful influence on a dog, especially when you are out and about in new or exciting areas, and sometimes a whistle will cut through to his sense of hearing more effectively than your voice. There are detailed step-by-step guides to training the recall with both voice and whistle, reinforcing the recall around distractions using a long line, and the more advanced chase recall, in *100 Ways to Train the Perfect Dog*.

We are often asked when exercising our own dogs why we continue to reward even the oldest dogs when they come straight back if called. The answer is simple: dogs work well and consistently if their effort is appreciated and rewarded. Once your dog understands the behaviour, save the best rewards for the fastest responses – give the occasional jackpot to teach him that it's worthwhile to keep listening for and responding quickly to your call.

If the recall ever slackens don't be afraid to go back and reinforce this important exercise with some line training.

TTouches

- *Mouth Work*
- *Ear Slides*
- *Zigzags*
- *Clouded and Lying Leopard TTouches all over the body*
- *Tail Work*
- *Python Lifts down legs*

It's not long before Marie is able to drop the line again and feel confident that Maisie will come immediately.

Maisie races in when called and slides to a halt.

USEFUL GROUND WORK EXERCISES

Different surfaces

Raised board

Labyrinth

She is confident that Marie will reward her red-hot recall.

Related ideas...   12   83   85   86

81 Chase drive

Sight hounds have been bred to catch fast-moving game, and herding breeds to chase and herd moving stock. They really excel at these jobs. However, most of us do not keep dogs to catch our dinner or round up sheep in the back garden.

It is important to teach your dog games that he can enjoy sharing with you by retrieving and returning specific articles. There are some great toys on the market that can be thrown a long way for dogs to chase, but you should also provide balance by teaching your dog to track or search.

Dogs with a high chase drive often lack focus, so working with recall and other training games, as well as ground work exercises, will help you to develop a good bond with your dog. Tension in the back and behind the shoulder blades can exacerbate barking and chasing and is present in most dogs that are constantly on the look out for prey. Use the TTouches listed here to keep your dog relaxed and to relieve tight muscles, and teach him the 'Look at me' exercise so that you can ascertain at which point he starts to lose his focus when out and about.

USEFUL GROUND WORK EXERCISES

Different surfaces

Raised or uneven poles

Fan

Archie loves to run: as a sight hound he was bred to chase.

Sarah has taught Archie to respond to a whisper, and also to the whistle, to get his attention when they are out walking in the fields, and his focus is no longer on squirrels and rabbits.

TTouches

- *Leg Circles*

- *Shoulder Lifts with wraps*

- *Python Lifts down the shoulders, along the back and down the front limbs*

- *Turtle TTouches on the shoulders and through the ribs*

- *Raccoon TTouches between and around the shoulder blades*

Related ideas...   80   85   86

Quad bikes

Dogs often learn to chase quad bikes, as well as other dogs, joggers, livestock, push-bikes and so on: all these moving targets offer the potential of a rewarding pursuit. Our aim is to alter the behaviour and help the dog to learn some self-control, rather than punishing him for wanting to pursue a specific object.

USEFUL GROUND WORK EXERCISES

Labyrinth

Different surfaces

Raised poles

Weave cones

Dogs adopt habitual postures when they are about to chase, and TTouch gives us the tools to change posture and a window of opportunity to modify behaviour. They often lose a sense of their body once instinct kicks in, and a body-wrap or T-shirt can help to restore awareness. A double connection, using a harness, collar and double-clipped lead, is ideal for helping your dog to stand in balance. It also enables you to contain your dog without resorting to force.

Try to establish what triggers the chasing behaviour: is it the movement of the vehicle, or its sight and sound alone? Work at an appropriate distance so that your dog is able to stand in a natural and relaxed posture on a loose lead. Use the clicker and treats to mark any calm behaviour. If the dog alters his posture and prepares to chase, quietly move him further away from the bike and help him to settle before continuing.

Case History
STANLEY

Stanley has developed the habit of chasing quad bikes and as he is a rescue dog his owners, Mike and Anne, will never know the original trigger for this behaviour. Stanley found it difficult to cope with the sight of a quad even though Marie was using TTouch, so we decided to remove the stimulus completely and started by teaching him to move slowly and in balance, combining body work with ground work exercises and the clicker.

The restriction of a lead can trigger more reactive and aroused behaviours, so we used a sliding line when we re-introduced Stanley to a static bike. He was able to calm down and focus on us and the rewards he was given. The clicker is invaluable for rewarding even the briefest shift of focus away from the quad bike, and Stanley responded so well that we were able to ask Jon to sit on the quad (without starting it) while we continued to work with Stanley. There is rarely an overnight cure for a long-standing problem, but with time Stanley will learn that it is more rewarding to ignore the quad bike.

TTouches

- *Ear Slides*

- *Raccoon TTouches around the shoulder blades*

- *Back Lifts*

- *Connected TTouches along the back*

- *Tail Work*

Stanley becomes very aroused by quad bikes, even if they are stationary.

When we brought the quad bike back out we used a sliding line to give Stanley a new experience.

Although Stanley looked at the quad bike when Jon got back on board, he chose to look away and was rewarded for this excellent behaviour.

Related ideas...   74   81   85

83

Car chasing

This is obviously a very dangerous behaviour, and needs to be resolved quickly. TTouch techniques can help a dog to learn self-control, and also creates the possibility for him to adopt a different posture, thus providing a different experience of cars passing.

It is perfectly natural for an owner to wrap a single lead round their hand and hold on tight to try and stop their dog from dragging them towards a moving car, but this gives the dog something to pull against and it does nothing to change his impulse to chase the car. Using a harness and a double-clipped lead, with one end attached to the harness and the other to a flat collar, gives you far more control with dogs that pull and lunge. Remember to use your clicker to mark and reward all calm behaviour.

Working down the legs and on the paws helps to ground dogs with a chase drive.

Working around the head helps to calm mental anxiety and arousal.

A T-shirt, harness and double-clipped lead, and a clicker are vital tools for helping dogs that chase.

TTouch work around the hindquarters will help to reduce tension in the body.

Related ideas... 81 82 86

Fear of traffic

If your dog is scared of traffic, use TTouch body work and ground work to improve his posture, confidence and awareness. Use a steady, calm tone of voice to talk to your dog. If you try to become too encouraging you may make him more afraid.

84

Find a place a little way from the traffic to sit and watch the world go by. Click and treat calm behaviour. Run through some tricks that your dog loves to perform at a safe distance from moving vehicles and gradually move closer. Some dogs can gain confidence standing behind a barrier or gate, so use your front garden and those of family and friends to build his confidence. A body-wrap or T-shirt may help him feel secure.

A supermarket carpark can be a good place to extend the exercise. Keep the session short to ensure that it is a good experience for your dog and so that he doesn't become overwhelmed. You can gradually pick busier times as your dog becomes more confident.

TTouches

- *Troika*
- *Ear work*
- *Mouth Work*
- *Chimp, then Raccoon around face, muzzle and base of skull*
- *Connected circles along the body and down the legs*
- *Tail work*

USEFUL GROUND WORK EXERCISES

Teeter totter

Labyrinth

Weave cones

Walking between barriers

Cuillin is watching the world go by from the safety of the gate. Tracey helps him remain calm with some Raccoon TTouches around his face and muzzle.

Related ideas... 81 82 83

Horses

A dog that is frightened or lacks confidence does not always cower away from the object of his concern, but may adopt a more defensive posture such as lunging and barking or even chasing. It is quite common for dogs to be nervy around horses, and to exhibit this behaviour. As this can be dangerous for horse, rider and dog, it is important that the issue is addressed.

Start by stroking your dog gently all over, noting areas where he is sensitive to contact, where the skin and/or muscles are tight or where there are temperature changes. Dogs with a high chase drive are usually tight through the shoulders, and dogs that are overly aroused by movement and noise are generally tight through the hindquarters.

Preparation at home

Use ground work at home in a controlled environment to improve your own posture and balance as well as your dog's. Use the clicker to mark his relaxed posture and work on the 'Look at me' exercise (see page 28) to encourage him to use his brain and to move through his neck and body. Get him used to wearing a half-wrap and a harness, as pulling on his neck with a collar will probably increase his arousal levels. Once you have mastered some quiet handling skills you can progress to the outside world.

Enlist the help of a friend who has a calm horse, or work with your dog outside a field of quietly grazing horses. The aim is to work in small, easy stages, where the stimulus can be controlled to some extent.

Stay as calm as you can. Gripping the lead too hard, holding your breath or bracing your own body will trigger more reactive responses in your dog. Watch your dog's posture for the point at which he starts to become overly concerned or aroused. This may be three fields or three metres away – it all depends on the dog. Stay below the threshold at which he reacts; you should be able to reduce the distance over a few sessions.

USEFUL GROUND WORK EXERCISES

Weave cones

Different surfaces

Raised poles

Labyrinth

Mark any relaxation with your clicker, as well as any appropriate behaviour such as standing quietly on a loose lead and watching the horse, or walking past without lunging. If he kicks off and starts leaping about and barking, or goes completely rigid and quiet, calmly lead him away. The moment he looks away from the horse, click and give him a treat.

Use your TTouches to show him how to relax his body and shift his focus, and/or set out some poles (or ropes, which can be easily transported) in a labyrinth so that your dog has something else to focus on.

Avoid rushing any of the steps and if necessary enlist the help of a trainer who uses the same or similar techniques. Have faith! Stay calm and enjoy the journey.

TIP

Be prepared for sudden noises or movement from the horse, and bear in mind it may be the sound of hooves on the ground or the horse's snorting that upsets the dog, and not just the visual stimulus.

Sarah starts working with Skipper and Meryl using TTouch body work and ground work exercises.

Case History

SKIPPER

Skipper came to live with Meryl and Trevor from a previous home where he had apparently been under-socialized. He was keen to chase horses and other livestock, and had issues with other dogs and people (including children).

They sensibly taught Skipper to wear a muzzle, and sought help from a local trainer who advocated all manner of useless techniques. Overwhelmed by his problems, they wondered if he was beyond help. Sarah worked with Skipper for one session and he made huge changes, no longer launching himself at other dogs. At a second session he was introduced to Marie and his local TTouch practitioner and dog trainer Garry Hinton, who continued to work with him. Skipper also came to Tilley Farm to work with horses for the photo-shoot for this section, and has never looked back.

As is usually the case, Skipper was fearful of hand contact from strangers. TTouch body work and ground work are vital in helping dogs to overcome such issues, and this was the starting point for Skipper.

Update by Meryl Collins

Dear Sarah

Skip has come such a long way since we first met you and the team at the Wag and Bone show we thought we would give you an update on his progress as we approach the end of the year.

We are no longer visiting Garry with Skipper because we don't need to!! We are now able to take him out without the muzzle and let him off lead in the company of other dogs. He plays happily with all sizes, colours and breeds and is even happy to share his toys (!!!!) but still returns to us when called. He also loves to swim in the ponds, even in the chilliest of weather. He also now stands quietly while horses with riders pass and (on the whole) ignores all the wild ponies and cattle grazing on the heath.

He allows us to hold his paws to trim his nails and happily stands to be bathed and groomed.

The opportunity to introduce him to children has been limited but he is firm friends with the eight-year-old daughter of a close friend of ours.

It truly was a fortuitous day when we met you and the team and we thank you from the bottom of our hearts, Skip means so much to Trevor and me. Having him around has helped me so much and he is now the root of so much fun and laughter in our home I can't bear to think that we were on the verge of having to re-home him when we met you.

Garry was wonderful with him – and us – and we learnt so much more that has been of help. We are looking forward to starting classes with him and trying to teach him all the skills in your great new book.

Fond regards Trevor, Meryl & Skipper xxx

She works around his head and his neck to reduce tension in his body.

A horse appears and Skipper's posture changes. If it is not safe to touch your dog when he is aroused use a fake hand to do the TTouches.

TTouches

- Relaxing TTouches all through the body
- Raccoon TTouches around the back of the skull and on either side of the head
- Back lifts with wrap or the flat of your hand
- TTouches around the hindquarters
- Python Lifts down legs
- Tail Work
- Ear Slides

Sarah progresses to working on his body with her hands.

Skipper lies down.

Sarah and Meryl walk Skipper, and Sarah rewards his calm behaviour and relaxed posture.

Even when the horse starts to move Skipper remains calm.

Related ideas...   81   86

Control around livestock

All dogs should be kept under control when around livestock. A farmer is within his rights to shoot any dog that is distressing his animals, and livestock chasing is extremely traumatic for the animals that are being pursued.

If dogs have a high chase drive, they can still pull you over or cause you a serious problem when on the lead so it is sensible to follow the same steps that we used with Skipper to teach your dog to behave appropriately around other animals.

Teach a good recall at home and use a whistle as shown in *100 Ways to Train the Perfect Dog* and find out what rewards are of high, high value to your dog. You are going to need them. Practise at home, in your garden and in a quiet environment using a long line.

Teach the chase recall exercise (also *100 Ways to Train the Perfect Dog*) and teach your dog to respond to a whisper. If you whisper his name when out and about he has to focus on you otherwise he might miss the treats.

Try to establish at what point he begins to get aroused and use your TTouches to reduce any bracing or tension in his body. Use a head collar in conjunction with a harness as shown in the photographs so that you can turn his head towards you if he starts to stare at the animals and fix through the body. Use the clicker to mark any calming in his behaviour.

Teach him to walk in a figure of eight on the lead at home or in the garden using cones and the clicker so that you can curve him away from the object of his affections.
If he is able to learn some self-control when passing livestock you can work with him on a long line in a similar way but be careful. If he is at the end of the line and is no longer focused on you, he may pull away if he suddenly comes upon a flock of sheep.

Leo has grown up around animals but as he hits adolescence his behaviour is changing. A combination of clicker training and TTouch are helping him to understand that quiet, controlled behaviour around all livestock brings him great rewards.

As Leo is already a very powerful dog, Sarah has taught him to wear a headcollar which will enable her to gently turn his head should the need arise. It is important that a double clipped lead is used with one end attached to a harness and the other end attached to the ring on the head collar. Using a head collar on its own will limit your ability to turn your dog away and may harm or panic him if he leaps and lunges.

TIP

Use the TTouches and ground work exercises recommended for working with horses.

Related ideas...   80   81   85

Fear of the car

Dogs can have problems with cars for several reasons. They may feel sick, be noise sensitive, have a negative association with a car or feel out of balance when it is moving. They may remember hurting themselves when they jumped into a vehicle, or they may have received a static shock when getting in or out of the car.

Think of anything you might be able to do to help your dog feel more comfortable in the car: expecting him to travel in a cramped crate or on a slippery seat is unfair. Consider investing in a car ramp (not too steep) or making a low-level boardwalk with a short ramp so that he can climb in easily. It also helps to open a window before you shut the door, to stop the air pressure hurting his ears.

As with any problem, break things down into tiny steps to make him understand that car travel is nothing to worry about. We usually start with the ground work exercises listed to improve balance and self-confidence. Put a doggy T-shirt or a half-wrap on your dog to give him better body and spatial awareness.

It goes without saying that the dog should not be dragged towards the car. If you have trained him to target a mat, place this near the vehicle. Be careful that you get your timing right and click and treat when the dog is approaching the car and not frozen or shaking with fear. Keep the sessions short and once he is confidently getting into the car, sit inside it with him and use your touches to keep him relaxed. Leave the doors open so that he does not feel trapped and avoid the temptation to go on a drive straight away.

Once your dog is happily getting into and sitting in the car, you can start going on short drives. Watch his responses to see if he becomes distressed and be prepared to go back a step if necessary. Keep thinking about the environment when on the move. You may need to open two windows if he needs air. Having only one window open will affect the air flow in the car and this may hurt your dog's ears.

Make sure the journey ends with a positive association, such as the park or a play date with other dogs. If you only ever drive him to the vet he is unlikely to be enthusiastic about car travel.

Sally is worried about getting in the car.

USEFUL GROUND WORK EXERCISES

Teeter totter

Uneven surfaces

Wobbly surfaces

Walking between barriers

Walking under plastic

Raised boards

TTouches

- *Ear Work*

- *Mouth Work*

- *Clouded Leopard TTouches over shoulders and hindquarters*

- *Tail Work*

- *Leg Circles*

- *Zigzags*

- *Wither rocking*

Teaching her to use a ramp gives her more confidence and enables us to break the exercise down into small steps.

Sally then plucks up the courage to jump in and out of the car unaided.

The ramp is a real help and Sally moves confidently into the car.

Tail Work helps to release tension in her hindquarters.

Related ideas...   54   88   89   90

88 Travel sickness

Car sickness is often linked to poor balance, and some dogs will grow out of it. However, for some dogs motion sickness and excessive salivation continue to be problems, but with careful planning there is a lot that you can do to help.

Avoid giving your dog a big meal before he travels, and check that he has room to move in his crate or can sit comfortably on the back seat. If you have trained him to lie down on a 'Settle' cue he will stay calmer than if he is constantly fidgeting in the car.

You may find it helpful to sit inside the car with him without actually travelling anywhere, particularly if your dog feels anxious about the car. When you do make a journey, keep it short and get someone else to drive if possible, while you perform Ear Slides on your dog. Put a half-wrap or T-shirt on him. Stay calm if he becomes anxious or is sick, as a fuss will increase his stress levels.

TIP

Use the TTouches and ground work exercises recommended for dogs that are reluctant to get in the car (see way 87).

Related ideas... 87 90

89 Getting out of the car

If your dog is reluctant to get out of the car, it may be because car rides always used to end up at the vet or dog shelter, or he may have been dumped at the roadside. He may have stiff joints, or the concussion on landing may cause him pain. To rule out any medical problem a trip to the vet is recommended.

Using a ramp, or a raised board with a low ramp at one end, will help your dog get out of the car. Put a harness on him so that you can support his exit from the vehicle if necessary.

Try doing some TTouch work on him before you ask him to leave the vehicle, to increase circulation and reduce any stiffness, and use a body-wrap to give him better body-awareness. Stroking him with a wand will also give him a better connection through the body.

TTouches

- Ear Slides
- Zigzags
- Lifts down legs (if you can access them!)
- Tail Work

USEFUL GROUND WORK EXERCISES

Teeter totter

Raised board

Different surfaces

Teaching your dog to walk over a teeter totter will give you valuable information about how he feels on a moving object and will also help him to develop better balance.

Related ideas... 87

Overexcitability and destructive behaviours in the car

The promise of an exciting game or walk at the end of the journey can be a trigger for overexcitability and destructive behaviours in the car, but these can also be the symptoms of a nervous dog that is stressed.

Whatever the cause of your dog's behaviour, the steps to helping him settle in the car are largely the same.

Use a body-wrap or T-shirt to help your dog settle and to feel more secure. A face-wrap or calming band (see page 38) often works like magic.

Teach him to lie down on a 'Settle' cue so that he is less aroused by visual stimuli outside the windows. If he is able to eat in the car, give him a Kong stuffed with yummy treats as a more appropriate outlet for his excitement.

Working over several sessions, sit with the dog in the car without the engine running and use TTouch work to keep him relaxed. TTouches and ground work exercises at home will improve his co-ordination and self-control.

Ask a friend to drive the car while you sit with your dog doing TTouches, and stay calm. If you are stressed your dog will know!

Excessive barking is very distracting for the driver and can be a sign of stress in the dog.

USEFUL GROUND WORK EXERCISES

Teeter totter

Labyrinth

Different surfaces

TTouches

- Ear Slides

- Mouth Work

- Python Lifts down all four limbs

- Tail Work

- Clouded Leopard TTouches around chest and hindquarters

- Lying Leopard and/or Clouded Leopard TTouches all over the body

The calming band can help dogs to settle and lie down.

Related ideas...   60   87   88

91 Make trips to the vet easier

A dog that dislikes being touched is probably going to resist being handled by a vet, although this is not always the case. Pain and fear can result in a negative association with the clinic, regardless of how caring and gentle the team have been during examination and treatment.

If your dog is reactive at the vet's you obviously need to muzzle him, and this will be far less worrying for your pet if you have taught him to wear his own muzzle on a regular basis (see page 29).

Use TTouches all over your dog's body to ascertain whether he has any sensitive or ticklish areas; you can also use them to help him stay calm in the waiting room to keep anxiety to a minimum. Ear Slides are fantastic for lowering heart rate and respiration, and a body-wrap can also be of benefit.

Sarah uses Clouded Leopard TTouches to help Cookie Dough to settle at the vets. Cookie is wearing a T-Shirt to help her stay calm and composed.

Related ideas...   13   33   52   54

92 Depression

It is not just humans that are increasingly suffering from depression. The modern dog can become depressed as well. Boredom, bereavement, change in circumstance and loneliness are probably the key reasons behind this sad condition, but it is also worth taking him to your vet in case he is quiet because he is unwell.

Stay positive. Feeling sorry for a depressed dog will probably make him feel worse. Dogs seem to pick up how we feel so stay positive as there is a lot that you can do to help regain your companion's zest for life. Use the TTouches listed to help him release tension, and try a half-wrap or doggy T-shirt to give him a sense of security.

Take him out and about. New sights and sounds will help him to regain an interest in life. If he doesn't want to walk, a drive in your car may cheer him up. Give him the opportunity to socialize with other dogs, unless he finds canine companionship a threat. Enrol in classes such as fun agility or dog games classes: dogs love to be successful and to learn new skills, just like people.

Choose any ground work exercises that will encourage your dog to be active, and encourage him to play shared games, including the interactive Nina Ottosson toys. You could even build him an activity centre in your garden. You are limited only by your imagination.

Bud came to live with Sarah as he was suffering from depression in his old home. He still sucks his bed but has stopped making holes in it and no longer cries all day.

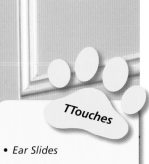

TTouches

- *Ear Slides*
- *Raccoon TTouches around the shoulders and withers*
- *Slow, connected Clouded Leopard or Lying Leopard TTouches all over the body*
- *Python Lifts down the front legs and along the neck and back*

Related ideas...   5   6   7

Rheumatism and arthritis

These conditions are common problems for older dogs, but young dogs can also suffer. Regardless of your dog's age, you can help him live a more comfortable life using TTouch in conjunction with appropriate veterinary care.

A warm, soft place to sleep and rest is a must for dogs with these diseases. We have found the cheapest way to provide wonderful squashy beds is by using single duvets folded into doggy quilt covers. In cold, damp weather a dog may wake more frequently and feel more uncomfortable once the heating has gone off, so invest in a fleecy dog coat or heat pad to keep him warm.

Ensure that your dog does not become overweight, as this will put more pressure on his joints and bones. Non-weight bearing exercise like hydrotherapy can help to keep the older dog fit and moving more easily. Talk to your vet about dietary supplements and pain relief.

Body work and ground work

TTouch is wonderful for stiff joints. It can help to relieve discomfort, and elderly dogs in particular will appreciate the special time you spend together.

Wearing a half-wrap for short periods can help improve a dog's movement, particularly when doing short ground work sessions, but if it looks as though his gait has become stiffer or more uneven, remove the wrap.

Keep body work and ground work sessions short. TTouch can have such a powerful impact that your dog may leap around with new-found vim and vigour, causing more discomfort later on.

She learnt a hand touch greeting and began to make new friends.

This little dog suffered from ill health when she was young and was under-socialized as a result. Illness and pain can greatly affect confidence and tolerance.

Marie was able to start some body work using the Chimp TTouch.

TTouches

- Clouded Leopard, Lying Leopard, Raccoon, Python Lifts, Connected Circles, Snail's Tail anywhere and everywhere

- Leg Circles, using false floor if necessary

Related ideas...

92

94 Loss of hearing and/or sight

A retractable lead can really be useful for an older dog with these problems, as it gives him a little freedom but also the security of a light connection with you. Your dog needs the opportunity to potter and sniff at his own pace but be careful that he does not get knocked over if you exercise him with boisterous younger dogs.

Try to be patient if your older dog appears to ignore you; he may be losing his hearing and may have already adjusted to respond primarily to your body language and signals. Make sure that he can see you when you want to communicate with him.

Continue with your TTouch work and use a half-wrap or doggy T-shirt to help him with his body-awareness. This is really important for dogs that are losing or have lost one or more of their senses.

Related ideas...   93   96   97

95 Topical treatments

Some dogs are natural wimps. You only have to *think* about removing a thorn or a grass seed to send them off to hide in a quivering heap, and if you actually *look* at the dog while you are wondering how to tackle the problem, your sensitive psychic is bound to protest.

The best way to work with dogs like these is to prepare in advance and accustom them to being TTouched all over their body, to wear a muzzle, and to respond to basic verbal cues such as 'Sit', 'Stand' and 'Lie down'. Teach them that it is safe to be stroked all over with the wand and habituate them to being touched with a wide variety of different objects, such as soft artists' water-colour brushes, wide feathers, wisps of straw, rubber groomers and cotton wool. (Obviously avoid anything that might hurt your dog.)

Pay attention to your own body posture at all times, and practise breathing when you work with your dog. If an animal has an injury, however minor, our own stress levels are affected and we are likely to hold our breath. The more relaxed we can be, and the more used to working with and handling dogs in a neutral situation, the calmer and more relaxed we can stay in times of trouble. This alone will go a long way to helping our troubled hounds.

USEFUL GROUND WORK EXERCISES

Different surfaces

Labyrinth

TTouches

- *Work all over the body using a variety of TTouches, including*
- *Raccoon TTouches around the feet*
- *Ear Slides*
- *Llama and Chimp TTouches*

TTouch work is fantastic for helping dogs to remain calm when being treated or checked over. It also enables you to touch areas that may be of concern to the dog and accustoms the dog to being handled all over his body.

Related ideas...   53   96   97

Eye medications

If you have a dog that is worried about eye medications, use Raccoon TTouches around his eyes, all over his head and around the base of the ears to start changing his expectation of what contact in these areas may mean.

This may take time, and it can be a good idea to incorporate these TTouch sessions into his daily walk, so that you do them when you are far removed from the room where the offending drops are administered.

Teach him to target (see page 29) and once he has mastered this skill take the medication outside and teach him to target the bottle. If he is unsure, teach him to target the back of your hand without holding the bottle, then hold the bottle and ask him to target your hand again. This will help him to associate medications with fun and games instead of something unpleasant.

Once he is happy with the TTouches and with targeting the bottle, use the bottle to do the TTouches around his body and around his face and/or head.

Experiment with applying the treatments while in different locations and re-read the section on Berserk Human Syndrome in the Introduction.

Teaching your dog to target medications can be a brilliant way of changing negative associations.

TTouches

- *Ear Work*
- *Mouth Work*
- *Chimp and Llama TTouches around the head and face*
- *Raccoon TTouches around the eyes*

TTouch work can be practised at any time and can be used before and after administering eye meds. It is also useful to teach your dog to be touched around the eye for easy bathing and the removal of any foreign objects.

Related ideas...

95   97

Ear medications

As with other topical treatments this can be a problem, particularly for dogs that have constant ear infections. Here again, TTouches can help to change your dog's expectation of contact around his ears.

Work on the dog's ear flaps, using your thumb to make circular TTouches, and build slowly to the point where you can do gentle Ear Slides. Use TTouches around his neck, along the base of the skull and around his muzzle. You can try a head wrap, but be careful not to force it on him if he is really sore.

Teach him to target the medicine bottle in the garden, when out on a walk and so on, to change his expectation of what the bottle means. Use high value rewards, so that he wags his tail when he sees the bottle instead of cowering and trying to slink away.

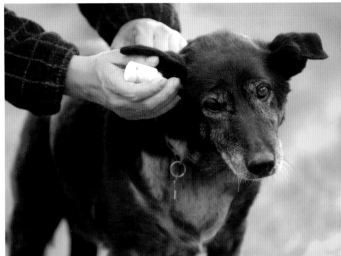

Ginny sometimes gets itchy ears and she knows when the drops are about to appear. Applying the drops when Sarah and Ginny are out and about helps to reduce Ginny's anxiety.

Use TTouches to help your dog enjoy rather than fear contact around his ears.

A good romp afterwards also stops Ginny sitting and scratching her ears and, although she can become a little defensive if she is in pain, Sarah has no problems popping in the drops, thanks to TTouch.

Do a little ear work before and after you administer ear drops.

Related ideas...   95   96

Issues with grooming

Dogs who have problems with grooming may have an old injury, or carry tension in their body and skin that makes grooming uncomfortable; they may have been accidentally hurt by a well-meaning person who was a little heavy handed; they may be fearful of contact, or simply find it hard to stand still.

The first step is to work all over your dog's body using the basic TTouches. If you cannot touch him on a part of his body it will usually follow that he will be wary of the brush and comb. Work slowly doing slides and circles with his hair if he is medium or long-coated, so that he becomes used to the movement of his hair. This will also help to reduce any tension in his skin. Continue with the TTouch sessions over several days if necessary, with the grooming equipment simply lying on the floor.

Gentle heat will help to relax tight muscles and skin. Heat a reusable hand warmer, pop it into an appropriate cover such as a thick woollen sock or mitten to reduce the heat a little, and use this to do slow TTouch work. If you don't have a hand warmer try warming a towel or your dog's favourite coat and do your TTouches through that.

Invest in a jelly scrubber and/or a sheepskin mitt. We use these a lot in our work and they provide the perfect stepping-stone for dogs that have issues with being groomed with a brush. Build gradually by doing the TTouches with the jelly scrubber and/or mitt and combining slow circular TTouches with a slow, light, sliding movement on the coat with the mitt and/or jelly scrubber. Once your dog is happy to be brushed with the jelly scrubber, repeat these steps with a soft body brush and continue until your pooch is spruced.

Pay attention to your own hand and arm and relax them – tension will make you work faster and with a heavier hand – and remember to listen to your dog. If he has poor balance, is old or has been unwell he may need to move about or lie down. You do not need to brush him all over in one go. Keep the sessions short and groom him over several days if he has any concerns.

Léo is typical of an adolescent male dog and is concerned about being groomed around the hindquarters. The jelly scrubber is a vital step towards helping him overcome any concerns that he may have.

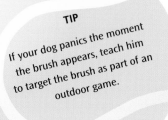

TIP

If your dog panics the moment the brush appears, teach him to target the brush as part of an outdoor game.

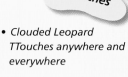

TTouches

- *Clouded Leopard TTouches anywhere and everywhere*
- *Hair Slides*
- *Ear Slides*
- *Tail Work*

Related ideas... 52 95 96 97

99

Bathing

Some dogs find water alarming. Or we should say clean, fresh water, as even dogs that freak when faced with the prospect of a bath usually enjoy wallowing in the swampiest, greenest muck. Even if you never plan on giving your dog a bath, there are times when his discovery of presents left by local wildlife might dictate the need for warm, soapy water. He may also need to be cooled if he overheats.

Use any opportunity to encourage your dog to be happy around water.

TIP

You can make the cleaning process even simpler by using warm, wet towels to loosen the dirt and an ionizing brush to groom your dog once his coat is dry.

Water play

Breaking down the bathing procedure into smaller steps may help your dog to accept this part of his care. Teaching him to play in water can be a useful step if he is really phobic about it. This will not only enrich his outside play, it will give you hours of fun as well. Use an old sand box, a child's paddling pool or even an old plastic dog bed, filled with a tiny amount of water initially, and see if he can discover it for himself. You can also try sitting some of his favourite toys in the water, but make sure he can pick them up without having to put his mouth in the water.

Walking on the beach or near a shallow stream will help, and if he has the company of a water-loving dog that's all the better.

After a short session using TTouch and the clicker and treats, Chloe remained totally calm when covered with the towel.

The beautiful Chloe likes to grab her towel the moment it appears. This is in part a puppy game but she is also over stimulated by contact on her body due to her age.

The bath

Once your dog is happy to stand in shallow water, you can progress to the bathtub. Groom any mats out of his hair before putting him in the tub, as the water will make them worse.

Put a large non-slip mat in the bottom of the bath and run a little lukewarm water before you take the dog into the bathroom. You may also want to fill a couple of buckets with warm water and have a plastic jug next to the bath, so that you can wet him thoroughly and rinse out the soap without turning on the tap.

Keep your hand contact soft when washing your dog and avoid gripping him too tightly. If your hand is heavy, your arm tense, or you rub him too vigorously, you may reinforce his fears. Talk to him in low, soothing tones. If you have an extra pair of hands to help, your assistant can do slow TTouch work around his chest and head while you are washing him. Keep the water away from his head, ears and eyes – wash his face separately with a wet face cloth later.

Wrap him in a towel before you lift him out of the bath, and gently rub the excess water from his coat, or use magic towels, which absorb excess water quickly.

TTouches

- Ear Slides
- Zigzags
- Tiger TTouch
- Python Lifts down leg

If he won't get in the bath

If you are unable to pick your dog up, or if he really panics in the bathroom, use buckets of warm water, a towel and a child's watering can in an enclosed area outdoors and build up his confidence slowly, in several sessions if necessary.

Teach him that a towel on his back is nothing to be concerned about, if necessary over a couple of sessions, and once he is happy to wear a towel pour a little water over it from the watering can. You can also make or buy a towelling coat, which will stay in place and can be used for drying him once he is happy with the concept of water. This will help to diffuse the sensation of water on his back.

USEFUL GROUND WORK EXERCISES

Different surfaces

Working between barriers

Related ideas...   72   98

100 Trim nails

Nail trimming can be a real nightmare if the dog has had a bad experience such as having the quick cut by mistake, or his paws have been held too tightly. Some dogs may have had their paws squeezed when they jumped up, setting up an issue with their feet, and others may have naturally sensitive and/or ticklish pads and toes.

If there is any chance that your dog will bite when you trim his nails, teach him to wear a muzzle (see page 29), but please do not use the muzzle as a free pass to force nail trimming upon him.

Break the sessions down into tiny steps to help him overcome his fears. Stroke him all over his body with a wand, and build his confidence gradually until you can stroke all four legs and his feet as well. Use Python Lifts on his shoulders and hindquarters.

Using the back of your hand, gently stroke down his legs. If he panics, go back to the point at which he remained calm and be prepared to work over several days.

Use the Chimp TTouch to work down his legs and around his feet.

Use a soft artist's paint-brush down his legs, on his feet and between his toes.

Poor balance and stiff joints can cause problems with nail trimming. Teach him to stand in balance by lifting each leg in turn without trying to hold on to the foot. Once he is happy for you to lift each leg, circle each leg slowly before placing the paw back on the ground.

Progress to Clouded Leopard TTouches down his legs and then Raccoon TTouches around his toes, but be prepared to build slowly over several sessions.

Get your dog accustomed to the noise of the clippers by clipping matchsticks or twigs and dropping or throwing him a treat each time you cut the wood. If he is phobic about nail-clippers, teach him to target them in a game, or try filing his nails using a Dremel instead.

Bud has really long nails that grow very quickly. They are also very tough which makes more noise when they are trimmed. The quick is also very long and Bud has been hurt by well meaning vets on many occasions. Sarah starting chunking the process down by using the clicker and treats combined with TTouch work.

It can be helpful to have someone assist you as you progress through the steps. Your assistant can use the clicker leaving your hands free to trim the nails.

USEFUL GROUND WORK EXERCISES

Different surfaces

Teeter totter

Related ideas...　52　96　97　98　99

Final Word

As always we have had great fun working together compiling this book. We hope that it has given you some inspiration as well as some useful tips and techniques to help you overcome any problems that you may be encountering with your dog.

Although we obviously have many years of experience we have every faith that you can help your dog to be happier, healthier and more content. As Linda says, we all have wonderful tools at our disposal; our eyes, our hands and our desire to make a difference to an animal's life.

Further information

About TTouch

TTouch was developed over 30 years ago by animal expert Linda Tellington Jones, There are over a thousand Tellington TTouch practitioners working in 27 different countries. It is used by a variety of dog handlers and trainers, including those working with service, competition and family dogs, veterinarians, dog walkers, groomers, shelter helpers, behaviour counsellors and veterinary nurses.

Further reading and educational CDs

100 Ways to Train a Perfect Dog
Sarah Fisher, ISBN 978-0-7153-2941-2
Unlock Your Dog's Potential
Sarah Fisher, ISBN 978-0-7153-2638-1
Getting in TTouch with Your Dog
Linda Tellington Jones, ISBN 1-872119-41-7
Clicker Training for Dogs
Karen Pryor, ISBN 1-86054-282-4
Haynes Dog Training Manual
Carolyn Menteith, ISBN 1-844253-51-1
The Canine Commandments
Kendal Shepherd, ISBN 978-1-874092-55-1
On Talking Terms with Dogs: Calming Signals
Turid Rugaas, ISBN 978-1929242368
Blue Dog Interactive CD is particularly good for teaching children about dogs. It is available from www.thebluedog.org, which also sells sound therapy CDs, see suppliers.

Suppliers

Jelly Scrubbers – www.tail-tamer.com also available in the UK
Kong toys – www.kongcompany.com for information on choosing and using these toys
Nina Ottosson Interactive toys – for a list of suppliers see www.nina-ottosson.com also available from www.companyofanimals.co.uk
Body-wraps and harnesses – available from www.ttouchteam.co.uk and www.ttouch.com

T-Shirts – the best fitting that we have found come from www.equafleece.co.uk
Fun training T-Shirts – www.K9byigloo.co.uk
Sound Therapy CDs – www.soundtherapy4pets.com
Training leads – www.ttouchteam.co.uk and www.companyofanimals.co.uk. Spiffy Dog Air Collars and Let'em Leads are available from www.spiffydog.co.uk
Training equipment – www.companyofanimals.co.uk. Mary Ray's Target, Click and Treat sticks are available from www.maryray.co.uk

Useful Addresses

Robyn Hood
TTouch Canada
5435 Rochdell Road
Vernon BC1VB 3E8
www.tteam-ttouch.ca

Linda Tellington Jones
TTouch USA
PO Box 3793
Santa Fe
New Mexico 87501
USA
www.ttouch.com

Eugenie Chopin
TTouch South Africa
www.ttouchsa.co.za

Sarah Fisher
TTouch UK
Tilley Farm,
Bath BA2 0AB
01761 471182
www.ttouchteam.co.uk
email: sarahfisher@ttouchteam.co.uk

Marie Miller
61 Grange Road
Longford
Coventry
West Midlands CV6 6DB
02476 366090
www.pawsnlearn.com
email: ttouch@pawsnlearn.com

Maria Johnston
13 Spa Lane
Hinckley
Leicester LE10 1JA
01455 457350

Association of Pet Dog Trainers
www.apdt.co.uk

Archie

I first met Archie whilst I was teaching a workshop at Battersea Dogs and Cats Home. He was petrified and in a terrible state, having been found as a stray a few days before. He came to live with my family in 2003 and had a multitude of problems including noise sensitivity, a high chase drive, timidity, stealing, counter surfing and issues in a car. Frankly the list was endless. With a combination of TTouch and clicker training he matured into a delightful and highly entertaining companion whom we all adored. He was diagnosed with cardiomyopathy in June 2009 and although the scans showed that he was responding well to treatment he died suddenly in his sleep a few weeks later, lying on his back in his bed with his glorious lurcher legs stretched up against the wall in his favourite position. I have so many wonderful memories of his life with us and am so very grateful for all that he taught me. Pay no attention to anyone who tells you it is impossible to teach a lurcher not to chase, using kind and gentle techniques. Archie learnt to sit and watch the wild rabbits playing on our lawn, had an excellent recall, and made us all laugh so much. His death was a total shock but I do believe that our dogs keep company with us until we reach our goals or we are ready to embark on a new chapter in our lives. This is certainly true for me and my family. The loss of a dog can be unbearable at times but I have had enough experience of death to know that we cannot influence the beginning or end of life. It is therefore important that we enjoy the times in between and take every opportunity we are given to learn from these wonderful beings that grace our lives. After all it is they, not us, who are the greatest trainers in the world.
Sarah Fisher

Acknowledgments

With thanks to Tina Constance, Robyn Hood, Linda Tellington Jones, Mags, Rachel, Harry and Monty Deness, Ryan Neile and the Blue Cross, Maria Johnston, North Road Vets Practice, Bob and Naomi Atkins, our editor Emily Pitcher (you are a star), Jon Langley and all the willing volunteers, both canine and human, who helped us to produce this book.

About the authors

Sarah Fisher is the UK's first TTouch Instructor and has worked with dogs for the past 15 years. She owns and runs Tilley Farm, which is home to the TTouch Training Programme in the UK. She has featured in many television programmes including *The One Show* (BBC1), *Animal Rescue Live* (BBC1) and *Talking to Animals* (ITV1 and Nat Geo). Sarah has contributed articles to many national and international magazines including *Your Dog* and *Dogs Today,* and is the author of *Unlock Your Dogs Potential* (D&C 2007) and the co-author of *100 Ways to Train the Perfect Dog* (D&C 2008). She teaches workshops for the UK's top shelters including Battersea Dogs and Cats Home and the Dogs Trust and lectures internationally and in the UK for a variety of organisations including the APDT and the International Companion Animal Welfare Conference. Sarah also fosters over-the-top puppies for Battersea Dogs and Cats Home and works with private clients on a one to one basis. She lives with her partner Anthony Head and their two daughters Emily and Daisy in a multi-dog household with Orsa, Léo, Ginny, Bud and Cookie.

Marie Miller has been working with dogs for the past 30 years and went on to establish Paws'n'Learn, her training and behaviour practice, in 1989. She is a TTouch Practitioner for Companion Animals and one of the founder members of the UK Association of Pet Dog Trainers. She has been the resident Pet Behaviourist and Trainer at Hollycroft Veterinary Centre, Hinckley, Leicestershire, for the past 19 years. Marie is also the Dog Editor for *Natural Horse Magazine*, and writes regularly for *Pet Products Magazine* and *Dog Trainer*. She lives with husband John, son Sean and dogs Fluffy, Tad, Oz, Maisie and Charlie.